HIS CROSS AND MINE

The Daily Cross

Lord, day by day I view Thy wondrous cross,
    The cross of Calvary;
And day by day I stretch my hands thereon,
    And die with Thee.

I "glory in the cross," most loving Lord,
    Because I know
It is the power to save and satisfy
    Where'er I go.

O gracious Lord, how sweet to take from Thee
    The daily cross,
And know I cannot separate forevermore
    Its gain and loss.

The daily cross is daily loss to all
    That keeps from Thee.
The daily cross is daily gain of all
    Thou art for me.

                  —*B. P. H.*

His Cross and Mine

By

Meade MacGuire

Author of "The Life of Victory"

TEACH Services, Inc.
PUBLISHING
www.TEACHServices.com • (800) 367-1844

Facsimile Reproduction

As this book played a formative role in the development of Christian thought and the publisher feels that this book, with its candor and depth, still holds significance for the church today. Therefore the publisher has chosen to reproduce this historical classic from an original copy. Frequent variations in the quality of the print are unavoidable due to the condition of the original. Thus the print may look darker or lighter or appear to be missing detail, more in some places than in others.

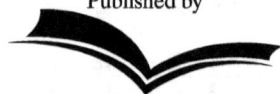

Copyright © 2024 TEACH Services, Inc.
ISBN-13: 978-1-4796-1207-9 (Paperback)

Published by

TEACH Services, Inc.
P U B L I S H I N G
www.TEACHServices.com • (800) 367-1844

CONTENTS

INTRODUCTION - - - - - - - 7

MY OWN CROSS - - - - - - 11

THE CROSS AND THE EARLY DISCIPLES - - - 17

THE CROSS IN HEAVEN - - - - - 21

THE CROSS SUPREME - - - - - - 29

GETHSEMANE - - - - - - 39

CALVARY - - - - - - - - 45

THE VICTORY OF THE CROSS - - - - 57

THE CROSS AND THE CRUCIFIXION - - - 71

THE CROSS AND SIN - - - - - 79

CRUCIFIED WITH CHRIST - - - - - 89

THE CROSS AND THE WORLD - - - - 97

THE FACE OF CHRIST - - - - - 111

The Old Rugged Cross

On a hill far away stood an old rugged cross,
   The emblem of suff'ring and shame,
And I love that old cross, where the dearest and best,
   For a world of lost sinners was slain.

Oh, that old rugged cross, so despised by the world,
   Has a wondrous attraction for me;
For the dear Lamb of God left His glory above,
   To bear it to dark Calvary.

In the old rugged cross, stained with blood so divine,
   A wondrous beauty I see;
For 'twas on that old cross Jesus suffered and died,
   To pardon and sanctify me.

To the old rugged cross I will ever be true,
   Its shame and reproach gladly bear;
Then He'll call me someday to my home far away,
   Where His glory forever I'll share.

So I'll cherish the old rugged cross,
   Till my trophies at last I lay down;
I will cling to the old rugged cross,
   And exchange it someday for a crown.
            —*George Bennard.*

INTRODUCTION

Many years ago I was passing through a large city, and, having a little leisure time, I determined to visit a museum of art where a collection of famous paintings was on exhibition. Friends had described with enthusiasm the wonderful masterpieces of art, and I anticipated a few hours of rare enjoyment. But I had come too recently from the majestic grandeur of the mountains, and the natural beauties of bird and blossom, of forest and stream, to be greatly fascinated by mere paintings of the landscape and nature, however beautiful.

I wandered about through the splendid galleries somewhat disappointed, until at length I found myself alone in a small room which contained, so far as I remember, but one painting. By this one my attention was instantly seized and irresistibly held. As I stood gazing upon the scene portrayed, it seemed to grow more and more real, till my heart almost stopped beating. It was a representation of the disciples removing the body of Jesus from the cross. The power of its realism fascinated me. It seemed as if I could almost hear the labored breathing of the men as they endeavored gently and tenderly to bear away that sacred form. It had fallen back limply into their arms. On that holy brow were traced in blood the jagged wounds made by the crown of thorns, and drops of blood had trickled down and dried upon His face. His nose and lips bore the pinched expression and the ashy hue of death. The hands and feet were lacerated, and a gaping wound showed where the spear had pierced His side, and the crimson stream from His broken heart had fallen to the ground and left a pool of blood at the foot of the cross.

All the teaching of twenty years concerning the sacrifice of Christ for sinners seemed to become concrete in a moment, and from my heart a hot, passionate cry arose, O my God, is it possible, can it be, that such a sacrifice was actually made to save a poor sinner like me?

Had this vivid consciousness of the reality of the cross as the price of my redemption been retained through all the succeeding years, how profoundly it must have affected my life. If it could today be made intensely real to all the disciples of Christ, how quickly it would transform a lukewarm, selfish, pleasure-loving church into that victorious body described by inspiration, "fair as the moon, clear as the sun, and terrible as an army with banners."

It is said that under the ministry of the early disciples five million souls were gathered into the church in one short generation. What mysterious secret did those men possess which swept away all barriers of religious prejudice on one hand, and pagan darkness and superstition on the other? Unquestionably it was the vivid sense of the reality of the cross. The disciples were clothed with the power of the omnipotent Spirit at Pentecost, because He is ever ready to possess those who are utterly yielded and committed to the work of exalting Christ crucified. When those men preached the gospel, their hearers beheld the scenes of the denial, rejection, condemnation, and crucifixion as vividly as if the events were transpiring in their very presence. Sinners quailed under the conviction of their awful crime, and cried for mercy and pardon. For this reason the apostle Paul was amazed that the people of Galatia, though but recently emerged from the darkness of heathen idolatry, should have been led astray by persecution or subtle temptation.

"O foolish Galatians, who hath bewitched you, that ye should not obey the truth, before whose eyes Jesus Christ hath been evidently set forth, crucified?"

The graphic word pictures of Paul, making real to

8

his hearers the thrilling scenes of Christ's atoning sacrifice, suggest the secret of the mighty power which attended his ministry.

Today many who call themselves Christians are repudiating those truths which are based upon the substitutionary work of Christ. To others is coming a new and more vivid revelation of the reality of the cross as the only hope of a lost world. This revelation is the result of a more thoughtful, prayerful study of the Scriptures, and more earnest contemplation of the scenes of Gethsemane and Calvary.

In this solemn hour the remnant people of God are represented in the Scriptures as the Laodicean church, as fallen into a state of spiritual lukewarmness and stupor, yet contented with the condition, reckoning themselves rich and increased with goods, and needing nothing.

O for a new revelation of the cross, a vision which will bring a deeper consciousness of the dreadful, malignant nature of sin, and of the infinite mercy and compassion of God! What a mighty change would appear should all believers heed the earnest appeal,

"When thou toilest, when thou sleepest,
When thou smilest, when thou weepest,
Or in mirth, or woe, hast part;
When thou comest, when thou goest,
Grief or consolation showest,
Hold the cross within thy heart."

Surely this would bring a deeper sense of human responsibility, and would result in a spiritual revival and reformation and evangelization in the church. God help us as individuals not to hesitate for some human leadership, nor tarry for some more powerful divine constraint, but without delay to prostrate ourselves before the cross, and seek a living union with the Crucified One. Then we may really "know Him, and the power of His resurrection, and the fellowship of His sufferings, being made conformable unto His death."

9

He Died for Me

I saw One hanging on a tree,
    In agony and blood;
He fixed His languid eyes on me,
    As near His cross I stood.

And never till my latest breath
    Can I forget that look!
It seemed to charge me with His death,
    Though not a word He spoke.

My conscience felt and owned the guilt,
    And plunged me in despair;
I saw my sins His blood had spilt,
    And helped to nail Him there.

Alas! I knew not what I did,
    But now my tears are vain;
Where shall my trembling soul be hid,
    For I the Lord have slain?

A second look He gave, which said,
    "I freely all forgive:
This blood is for thy ransom paid,
    I die that thou may'st live."

Oh, can it be, upon a tree
    The Saviour died for me?
My soul is thrilled, my heart is filled,
    To think He died for me.

                        —*John Newton.*

MY OWN CROSS

"All the grace which Jesus the saving one gives, is given only in the path of fellowship with Jesus the crucified one. Christ came and took my place; I must put myself in His place, and abide there. And there is but one place which is both His and mine,—that place is the cross. His in virtue of His free choice; mine by reason of the curse of sin. He came there to seek me; there alone I can find Him. When He found me there, it was the place of cursing; this He experienced, for 'cursed is everyone that hangeth on a tree.' He made it a place of blessing; this I experience, for Christ hath delivered us from the curse, 'being made a curse for us.'

"When Christ comes in my place, He remains what He was, the beloved of the Father; but in the fellowship with me He shares my curse and dies my death. When I stand in His place, which is still always mine, I am still what I was by nature, the accursed one, who deserves to die; but as united to Him, I share His blessing, and receive His life. When He came to be one with me, He could not avoid the cross, for the curse always points to the cross as its end and fruit. And when I seek to be one with Him, I cannot avoid the cross either, for nowhere but on the cross are life and deliverance to be found. As inevitably as my curse pointed Him to the cross as the only place where He could be fully united to me, His blessing points me to the cross, too, as the only place where I can be united to Him. He took my cross for His own; I must take His cross as my own; I must be crucified with Him.

11

It is as I abide daily, deeply, in Jesus the crucified one, that I shall taste the sweetness of His love, the power of His life, the completeness of His salvation."—*Andrew Murray, "Abide in Christ."*

———

It may be a surprising fact to many that Jesus never once spoke of the cross as His, but always as ours. The cross is mentioned in the New Testament twenty-seven times. Of this number, five are attributed to Jesus. Apart from the words of Jesus, Matthew records the expression three times, Mark three times, Luke once, John four times, and Paul eleven times.

We do not mean to imply that it would not be proper to speak of it as Christ's cross, for Paul uses the expression "His cross" once, "the cross of Christ" three times, and "the cross" seven times. We know that the words of Scripture are chosen with a divine purpose, and we may therefore infer that there is some important lesson to be learned from the very words Jesus used when He spoke of the cross. Here are the five passages recorded; let us consider them prayerfully, seeking to know their meaning to us:

"He that doth not take *his* cross and follow after Me, is not worthy of Me." Matt. 10:38, A. R. V.

"Then said Jesus unto His disciples, If any man would come after Me, let him deny himself, and take up *his* cross, and follow Me." Matt. 16:24.

"He called unto Him the multitude with His disciples, and said unto them, If any man would come after Me, let him deny himself, and take up *his* cross, and follow Me." Mark. 8:34.

"He said unto all, If any man would come after Me, let him deny himself, and take up *his* cross daily, and follow Me." Luke 9:23.

"Whosoever doth not bear *his own* cross, and come after Me, cannot be My disciple." Luke 14:27.

In every instance Jesus is talking about the great crisis in a man's life, when he is deciding the solemn question of his eternal destiny. There the man's *own cross* stands at the parting of the ways. Every rational human being faces the question, Shall I live for self or for God? You may say, The Christian life seems narrow, the way strait. Surely this is true, and it is your cross standing at the gateway which makes the road narrow and exclusive. There is a world of meaning in that brief sentence, "Let him deny himself, *take up his cross,* and follow Me."

"Jesus, I *my* cross have taken,
  All to leave and follow Thee;
All things else I have forsaken,
  Thou henceforth my all shalt be:

"Perish every fond ambition,
  All I've sought, or hoped, or known;
Yet how rich is my condition,
  God and heaven are still my own."

How often we have sung, "Jesus, I *my* cross have taken," with very little realization of the significance of the words! Or we have regarded the endurance of little daily trials and annoyances and self-denials, as taking up our cross and following Him.

God gave to mankind His great moral law, a law of love, which is holy and just and perfect. We have all transgressed that law, and as sinners are under the condemnation of death. We deserve to die. Should we perish on the cross, we would but receive what we justly merit. Therefore the cross belongs to mankind. It is your cross and mine.

Adam stood as the head and representative of the human race. He disobeyed God, and brought the condemnation of death upon himself and the whole human family. There was no possible escape through any means that man could devise.

But God had already provided a plan to meet the great emergency. Christ was to come to this world to redeem the lost race. To do this it was necessary

13

for Him to become one of us, to be born into the family. Then, standing in the place of Adam as the representative of humanity, He proposed to pay the penalty of the broken law, and win back what Adam lost.

Jesus took a human body, and a personality, the same as ours. He was subject to the same trials and sorrows, the same weariness, difficulties, hardships, and temptations. Yet He never in the slightest particular transgressed one precept of the divine law. His life was one of perfect obedience, unmarred by the least deviation from the path of holiness. Thus by His own character wrought out in frail humanity He merited eternal life and blessedness, even though He had been but a man. But He was vastly more than a man; He was "the Son of man." The significance of this title, which He seemed to prefer to all others, makes Him more than the son of *a* man. He was the typical, all-inclusive representative of all mankind. As such, the righteousness which He wrought out in His own life was sufficient for the whole race which He represented.

But before a sinner could appropriate this righteousness, satisfaction must be made to the divine law for his sins. Eternal justice demanded the death of the sinner. Christ had provided righteousness for every sinner, but what would it avail, since the sinner's life was forfeited? This is why Jesus died on *my* cross. In order to save me from the death which would inevitably have been eternal, He took my sins, and then my cross belonged to Him. Not as a man, but as the Son of man, the representative of the race, the voluntary substitute for every human being, standing in the place of each individual,—standing in my place,—He went to my cross and bore my sins in His own body on the tree.

The divine law set up a cross, and demanded that I, the sinner, be placed upon it to suffer my just deserts. But my compassionate Saviour said, "If you go to your cross, you will perish eternally. I will go in your place. I will shed My blood and lay down My life to atone for your sins."

The sufferings and death of Christ on the cross were in no sense related to His life. He had lived the life of a saint. Now He died the death of a sinner. It is evident, therefore, that whatever merit He acquired by His voluntary sacrifice on the cross, is His to impute to those who need it. And we need it. He was not enduring the sorrow and anguish because of any fault of His own. His were vicarious sufferings, through which He obtained a merit which He did not need for Himself. He took all my sins, and paid the penalty, fully satisfying the demands of the broken law against me. Thus He, standing as my substitute and recognized by the law as the representative sinner, gained a standing of justification before the law. This He now freely offers to me. The moment I accept Him as my sin bearer and Lord, He imparts this justification to me. The law then has nothing against me. I am free from its condemnation. The sentence of death is removed, and I am given a standing before God and His law just as if I had never sinned.

I realize that all this is mine only because Christ was willing to make the infinite sacrifice of making my cross His own. By acknowledging this cross as mine, I identify myself with Him in the utter renunciation to death of sin and the sinful nature. "Being justified freely by His grace," I "have peace with God through our Lord Jesus Christ." In Him I now have eternal life.

The two supreme gifts of God to man are LIFE and RIGHTEOUSNESS. The life, Christ purchased on the cross. The righteousness He wrought out in His earthly life. On the cross He took our death penalty for sin, thus removing our guilt and reconciling us to God. In His earthly life He perfectly wrought out the will of God in our human flesh, and this perfect obedience, or righteousness, He imparts to every true disciple.

"If, when we were enemies, we were reconciled to God by the death of His Son, much more, being reconciled, we shall be saved by His life."

The only way I can truly acknowledge Jesus as my Saviour is by taking up *my* cross. Thus I acknowledge my own guilt and condemnation. Thus I show my faith in His atoning sacrifice. Thus I demonstrate my confidence in the efficacy of His death to purchase life for me. Thus I enter into a living union with Christ, which provides emancipation from the dominion of sin, and secures to me the righteousness of Christ.

Tenderly

TAKE from the cross the dear form of the Master;
   Gently remove ye the nails from His hands;
Carefully cover the poor, mangled body,
   Loosen the cruel cords, sever the bands.

Take the rough crown from His pale, bleeding temple,
   Wash the dark stains from His dear, sacred head;
Tearfully weep o'er the blessed Redeemer,
   Tenderly bathe ye the wounds of the dead.

Fold ye the hands that so often in kindness
   Healed, as by magic, the woes of mankind,
Ministered oft to the poor and the needy,
   Strengthened the sick, and gave sight to the blind.

Tenderly bear Him, the crucified Saviour;
   Lift from thy spirit its terrible gloom;
Leave Him to rest; for the heavenly watcher
   Waits but to call Him to life from the tomb.

—*Mrs. L. D. A. Stuttle.*

THE CROSS AND THE
EARLY DISCIPLES

On the night before the crucifixion, when the Passover supper had been eaten, the little group in the upper room sang a hymn and went out unto the Mount of Olives. The Saviour revealed to His disciples that the night had come when the Scripture would be fulfilled, "I will smite the Shepherd, and the sheep of the flock shall be scattered." This sorrowful disclosure was followed by the assurance, "After I am raised up, I will go before you into Galilee."

In a few brief hours the disciples were plunged into a world of sorrow which they had not anticipated. Though Jesus had told them exactly what would take place, they seemed unable to comprehend His meaning, and the crucifixion came as an overwhelming surprise and disappointment. The resurrection seemed equally incomprehensible at first; nevertheless, when the time came, they "went into Galilee, unto the mountain where Jesus had appointed them."

After assuring them that "all power" "in heaven and in earth" had been given Him, the Master said, "Go ye therefore, and teach all nations." While Jesus lay in the tomb, their hopes and aspirations had died; but in the presence of the risen Lord hope revived, and they were filled with an intense desire to uplift Him before men as the Lamb of God, the Saviour of the world.

"Then opened He their understanding, that they might understand the Scriptures, and said unto them,

Thus it is written, and thus it behooved Christ to suffer, and to rise from the dead the third day: and that repentance and remission of sins should be preached in His name among all nations, beginning at Jerusalem."

Thus the Saviour summed up in a few simple words the gospel which was made known by all the inspired writers, and which is the power of God unto salvation to everyone that believeth—Christ, the atoning sacrifice, suffering, dying, rising again the third day, and ascending to the right hand of God to minister repentance and remission of sins. This was their message. It is the everlasting gospel, "the mystery brooded in the mind of the Infinite from times eternal." Waiting a few days in Jerusalem for earnest preparation of heart and the promised enduement of divine power, they went forth as witnesses to deliver the message entrusted to them.

As we read the record of those early days of irresistible triumph, we have no difficulty in discovering the secret of their success. The emphasis was all on the crucified, risen, and glorified Lord. Under the mighty dynamic of the Pentecostal outpouring the apostle set forth the guilt of all men incurred by the crucifixion of Christ.

"Ye men of Israel, hear these words: Jesus of Nazareth, a man approved of God among you by miracles and wonders and signs, which God did by Him in the midst of you, as ye yourselves also know: Him, being delivered by the determinate counsel and foreknowledge of God, ye have taken, and by wicked hands have crucified and slain." "Therefore let all the house of Israel know assuredly, that God hath made that same Jesus, whom ye have crucified, both Lord and Christ."

As that great audience were by this solemn charge brought face to face with their personal responsibility and guilt, they were seized with an awful sense of condemnation.

"Now when they heard this, they were pricked in

their heart, and said unto Peter and to the rest of the apostles, Men and brethren, what shall we do?" "Then they that gladly received his word were baptized: and the same day there were added unto them about three thousand souls."

Christ was set forth as the one whom they had crucified, the one who had risen and ascended to the right hand of God, the one who would grant mercy and pardon to the penitent. Men were convicted, they repented, and rejoiced in deliverance from the guilt and condemnation of sin.

This is the divine plan. Even before the haughty priests and rulers the disciples had no other message. When they were brought before the council, the high priest demanded, "Did not we straitly command you that ye should not teach in this name? and, behold, ye have filled Jerusalem with your doctrine, and intend to bring this man's blood upon us."

To this Peter boldly replied, "We ought to obey God rather than men. The God of our fathers raised up Jesus, whom ye slew and hanged on a tree. Him hath God exalted with His right hand to be a Prince and a Saviour, for to give repentance to Israel, and forgiveness of sins."

Again the rulers, elders, and scribes, filled with bitter hatred against the followers of Christ, were gathered together, and brought the disciples before them for examination. They asked, "By what power, or by what name, have ye done this?"

"Then Peter, filled with the Holy Ghost, said unto them, Ye rulers of the people, and elders of Israel, if we this day be examined of the good deed done to the impotent man, by what means he is made whole; be it known unto you all, and to all the people of Israel, that by the name of Jesus Christ of Nazareth, whom ye crucified, whom God raised from the dead, even by Him doth this man stand before you whole."

The method of those early disciples was twofold—they emphasized the terrible crime of men in putting to death the one who by supernatural signs and miracles of healing was so clearly demonstrated to be the Son of God. Men were seized with an awful sense of guilt and condemnation, and many were filled with sorrow and remorse.

Over against this the disciples exalted the Crucified One as the Lamb of God that taketh away the sins of the world, and held out to repentant sinners the offer of mercy and pardon through the shed blood of Jesus. Peter in his epistle said, "The burden of our sins He Himself carried in His own body to the cross, and bore it there, so that we, having died so far as our sins are concerned, may live righteous lives."

These humble men who wrought such mighty achievements in the face of national religious prejudice and bigotry, and later against a world entrenched in almost universal idolatry, were not contending for a theory, a creed, or a sect. They proclaimed a crucified and risen Saviour; not a mighty monarch, or even a pretender to an earthly throne, but one despised and rejected of men, cruelly persecuted and publicly executed between two criminals, but now resurrected and ascended to the right hand of God.

It was the mysterious power which attended this message that grappled with the darkness and degradation of the ages, and delivered millions from death.

THE CROSS IN HEAVEN

One of the great secrets of the fascination of the Bible is that it is all written with the purpose of revealing to humanity a glorious Person. How much many of us have missed by reading the Scriptures to discover some theory, or establish some doctrine, or produce some argument! Even when we apprehend an interesting truth, it is abstract, and lacks life-giving power, unless we learn "the truth as it is in Jesus."

The Saviour said, "Search the Scriptures; for . . . they are they which testify of *Me*."

When we open the word of God, we shall understand it only as we apprehend its relation to the character, or attributes, or office, or ministry of Jesus Christ. Not that He is seeking to hide from us or elude our approach, but He is infinite in wisdom and power and love, and hence must reveal Himself in a myriad aspects in order that we may have any true conception of what He is. There is not a book in the Bible that does not reveal Him. Some are simple and easily understood; others are deep, and require profound study and meditation.

We are but finite creatures, and can never fully comprehend His greatness; but as we search His word reverently and prayerfully, the Holy Spirit reveals to us more and more of the inexhaustible riches of His grace. God is love. We have no true knowledge of God unless our supreme thought of Him is that He is a God of love.

God manifested His infinite love in the gift of His

only-begotten Son to a race of sinners. The supreme revelation of that divine love which withheld not its all, but freely gave Him for our ransom, is the cross. Hence the cross is the central point in the revelation of God to man, and in the plan of human redemption.

As we study the word of God to obtain a fuller knowledge of the person of Jesus, the inspired writers are ever pointing us to the cross. Thus we come to understand that, "to be rightly understood and appreciated, every truth in the word of God, from Genesis to Revelation, must be studied in the light that streams from the cross of Calvary."

The Gospel narratives unfold to us the earthly life and ministry of Jesus culminating in His death on the cross. The last book in the Bible opens in our wondering gaze marvelous revelations of our ascended and glorified Lord. There He is clothed with infinite majesty and power, surrounded by the unnumbered hosts of celestial beings who comprise the principalities and powers of the heavenly world. But as the character of Christ shines more resplendently in the light of heaven, so also does the cross of Calvary.

The book opens with the words, "The Revelation of Jesus Christ." Immediately a blessing is pronounced on him "that readeth, and they that hear the words of this prophecy, and keep those things which are written therein." As we proceed to study it, we are astonished to see how every page is permeated and dominated by this glorious Person. In the very first chapter His name or a personal pronoun referring to Him occurs thirty-eight times (A. R. V.); in the second chapter, forty-two times; and in the third chapter, forty-seven times—one hundred twenty-seven times in seventy-one verses.

Moreover, these chapters emphasize constantly that while He is now the ascended and glorified Lord, He is still and forever the one who died on Calvary. In the very introduction He reveals Himself as "the first begotten of the dead," and the one who "loved us, and

washed us from our sins in His own blood." In verse
7 He tells of His coming in glory, when "every eye
shall see Him," including those also who "pierced
Him."

Then comes the description of His personal appearance in glory so overwhelming that the beloved
disciple "fell at His feet as dead." How startling and
how comforting are the next words! Jesus, the King
of glory, stooped to lay His right hand upon John, and
reminded him of the cross. "Fear not; I am the first
and the last: I am He that liveth and was dead."
It is as if He had said, Fear not, John, though you
hardly recognize Me clothed with divine glory and
majesty, I am the same Jesus on whose bosom you
reclined, the one who hung upon the cross, and who
gave His life for sinners. Now I am alive forevermore,
and have the keys of hell and of death.

In holy vision John was permitted to view many
scenes as the divine purposes were unfolded in heaven.
Doubtless to his surprise and wonder it seemed that
the fallen race on our little world occupied the attention of all heaven, and that the activities of the
heavenly host centered around man's Redeemer and
the mediatorial work in which He is engaged for man's
salvation.

In the fourth chapter John begins the description
of one of the most dramatic and thrilling of these
heavenly visions. "Straightway I was in the Spirit:
and behold, there was a throne set in heaven, and
One sitting upon the throne." About this exalted
throne of the Infinite, which was shrouded in ineffable
glory, were placed twenty-four other thrones, occupied
by twenty-four elders arrayed in white garments. On
the four sides of the throne were four living creatures,
apparently companies of the redeemed who were raised
with Christ at His resurrection, and ascended with
Him as trophies of His victory over sin and death.
Now, observe:

1. *The Book.*—"I saw in the right hand of Him that

sat on the throne a book written within and on the back side, sealed with seven seals." Rev. 5:1.

We may infer that it is the will of God to make revelations of His purposes from time to time to the inhabitants of heaven, that He may have the complete sympathy and intelligent co-operation of the angels, whom we are told are "all ministering spirits, sent forth to do service for the sake of them that shall inherit salvation." In His right hand is held a book. New mysteries relating to His eternal plan are about to be unfolded.

2. *The Challenge.*—"I saw a strong angel proclaiming with a loud voice, Who is worthy to open the book, and to loose the seals thereof?" Verse 2.

The interest of all heaven was centered in the book. A mighty angel came forth, and with a loud voice which reached to the farthest circle of the angelic throng he challenged any being in the universe to enter into the counsels of the Almighty.

3. *Silence.*—"And no man in heaven, nor in earth, neither under the earth, was able to open the book, neither to look thereon." Verse 3.

Why is this scene enacted in heaven? Evidently God chose in this way to glorify His beloved Son. Ages before, one of the most exalted beings in heaven had been jealous of the Son of God. He had been determined to thrust himself into the counsels of the Deity, and usurp the place belonging to the eternal Son alone. He was cast out of heaven, and introduced the same spirit of rebellion into this world. The Son of God came down to earth and died to redeem the race that was lost. He returned to His place at the right hand of the throne on high, and now the Father is giving the whole unfallen universe a striking lesson of the exalted position occupied by His victorious Son, who is to be honored and adored above all others.

4. *The Sorrow.*—"And I wept much, because no man was found worthy to open and to read the book, neither to look thereon." Verse 4.

24

All is breathless silence as every eye watches intently for an answer to the challenge. May not some glorious seraphim, standing high in the counsels of God, be able to open the book? Every voice is hushed; no being presumes to venture into that realm which the mind of the Infinite alone has explored. The suspense becomes too great for the poor trembling man who stands alone, a mortal, finite man in this great heavenly assembly. He feels that the destiny of his fellow men is concerned, and, fearing that the contents of the book are to remain forever sealed, he bursts into tears.

5. *The Assurance.*—"And one of the elders saith unto me, Weep not: behold, the Lion of the tribe of Judah, the Root of David, hath prevailed to open the book, and to loose the seven seals thereof." Verse 5.

How beautiful and comforting is this scene! One of the glorified elders, himself redeemed from among men, came to John and gave him the loving assurance that one had prevailed to open the book. John's weeping ceased, and he faced the scene again, eagerly looking for the Lion of the tribe of Judah.

6. *The One Who Prevailed.*—"I beheld, and, lo, in the midst of the throne and of the four beasts, and in the midst of the elders, stood a Lamb as it had been slain." Verse 6.

How striking is this symbolic title, "The Lamb," which occurs no less than twenty-six times in the book of Revelation. It is "the Lamb slain from the foundation of the world." It is the Lord Jesus Christ in heaven, exalted above every name that is named, adored by all the heavenly throng, yet still bearing in His body, unhidden by the transcendent radiance, the awful marks of Calvary. Those scars are His eternal glory, for they bear everlasting witness to the depth and faithfulness of His love.

7. *The Worship.*—"When he had taken the book, the four beasts and four and twenty elders fell down before the Lamb, having every one of them harps,

and golden vials full of odors, which are the prayers of saints." Verse 8.

How fitting that those who through the atoning sacrifice of Christ had entered into the joy of the eternal world, should prostrate themselves before the Lamb in grateful adoration!

8. *The Song.*—"And they sung a new song, saying, Thou art worthy to take the book, and to open the seals thereof: for Thou wast slain, and hast redeemed us to God by Thy blood out of every kindred, and tongue, and people, and nation." Verse 9.

The theme of this song should stir the heart of every child of Adam. It is the theme which alone can express the joy and gratitude of the redeemed; the theme which thrills the myriads of unfallen angels; the song which rejoices the heart of the Omnipotent One, the song of praise to the Lamb who poured out His life to atone for the sins of a perishing world.

9. *The Angels.*—"I beheld, and I heard the voice of many angels round about the throne and the beasts and the elders: and the number of them was ten thousand times ten thousand, and thousands of thousands; saying with a loud voice, Worthy is the Lamb that was slain to receive power, and riches, and wisdom, and strength, and honor, and glory, and blessing." Verses 11, 12.

So thrilling was the song of the redeemed that the angels of heaven could not keep silence, but burst into rapturous praise to the Lamb that was slain. And in the midst of this amazing drama the song was caught up in an ever-widening circle; "and every creature which is in heaven and on the earth, and under the earth, and such as are in the sea, and all that are in them, heard I saying, Blessing, and honor, and glory, and power, be unto Him that sitteth upon the throne, and unto the Lamb forever and ever." Verse 13.

This is the theme of heaven's song and the motive of heaven's activities—THE LAMB THAT WAS

SLAIN. Thus fully does the Lamb occupy the center of all those thrilling and dramatic pictures which set forth heaven's interest in this world and the salvation of sinful men. The inhabitants of heaven and of unfallen worlds find in the death of Christ on Calvary a subject of surpassing interest, a theme whose absorbing fascination never wanes through the passing of centuries and millenniums.

How little we realize what the cross means to the whole universe outside of our little world! We are filled with awe as we read what we can only faintly understand of the relation it sustains to the inhabitants of heaven and the millions of unfallen worlds.

"Moreover He is the head of His body, the church. He is the beginning, the first-born from among the dead, in order that He Himself may in all things occupy the foremost place. For it was the Father's gracious will that the whole of the divine perfections should dwell in Him. And God purposed through Him to reconcile the universe to Himself, making peace through His blood which was shed upon the cross—to reconcile to Himself through Him, I say, things on earth and things in heaven."

The sympathy awakened by Lucifer in his rebellion in heaven brought perplexity and misunderstanding, but through His blood Jesus reconciled the whole vast universe, binding them forever to the heart of God.

Jesus giving His life on Calvary for rebellious, degraded, degenerate men and women was the true revelation of the character of His Father. It not only refuted Satan's charge that God was selfish and arbitrary, but it exhibited His infinite compassion and love and self-denial.

From eternal ages God had looked forward to that hour when through the voluntary sacrifice of His Son all the created intelligences should know and understand, and love Him better. The astronomers tell us that there are at least five hundred millions of planets and stars, worlds and suns. Christ the Son of God

27

made them all, and was the adored Commander and King of all that vast creation. Yet He humbled Himself as a servant, and became obedient unto death, even the death of the cross. All these unfallen beings looked upon the cross with unbounded amazement. Even the Father, looking upon the sufferings which His Son endured, witnessed the most sublime moral act of the universe. It marked the focal point of eternity past and future. That hour when the expiring Son of God cried out with a voice which "seemed to resound through all creation," "It is finished," was not only the supreme hour for the human race, but the most sublime moment for the whole intelligent universe.

Is it not fitting that we in whose behalf this divine sacrifice was made, should regard it as the supreme subject to which all other things in this life should be subordinate?

THE CROSS SUPREME

"If those who today are teaching the word of God, would uplift the cross of Christ higher and still higher, their ministry would be far more successful. If sinners can be led to give one earnest look at the cross, if they can obtain a full view of the crucified Saviour, they will realize the depth of God's compassion and the sinfulness of sin.

"Christ's death proves God's great love for man. It is our pledge of salvation. To remove the cross from the Christian would be like blotting the sun from the sky. The cross brings us near to God, reconciling us to Him. With the relenting compassion of a Father's love, Jehovah looks upon the suffering that His Son endured in order to save the race from eternal death, and accepts us in the Beloved.

"Without the cross, man could have no union with the Father. On it depends our every hope. From it shines the light of the Saviour's love; and when at the foot of the cross the sinner looks up to the One who died to save him, he may rejoice with fullness of joy; for his sins are pardoned. Kneeling in faith at the cross, he has reached the highest place to which man can attain."—*Mrs. E. G. White, "The Acts of the Apostles," pp. 209, 210.*

———

Though the apostle Paul did not witness the crucifixion of Christ, it is evident that the revelation made to him at his conversion, together with information he received from eyewitnesses, made it absolutely real to

29

him. He mentions the cross more frequently than any other inspired writer. It is ever the center of his teaching and the recognized source of his power to win men.

Paul had been instrumental in establishing a church at Corinth, and in writing his first letter to them he said: "I determined not to know anything among you, save Jesus Christ, and Him crucified."

Should any man today make such a broad, sweeping statement, he might be regarded as rash or fanatical, but divine inspiration never dictated anything exaggerated or extreme. The subject is fully as important as this striking statement indicates. In making this declaration, Paul gives the key to his great career and the undying influence of his life. In the first chapter of the same letter he wrote, "We preach Christ crucified." His message did not consist of speculative theories about a "historical Christ" or an "ideal man," but was the exaltation of a crucified and risen Saviour.

Paul was a man of extraordinary learning, possessing by nature great intellectual ability, and having the best facilities of his time for acquiring knowledge. Though but a young man (when he enters the Scripture narrative), he had attained a place of honor and influence in his own nation. He was an author, an orator, a teacher, a statesman, a philosopher. One of the world's eminent scholars recently wrote, "The book of Romans is the most sublime masterpiece of all literature."

Above all philosophy, all science, and all other learning of this world, Paul exalted the knowledge of Christ crucified as the one supreme and indispensable truth. Weymouth's translation renders his statement, "I determined to be utterly ignorant, when among you, of everything except of Jesus Christ, and of Him as having been crucified."

Paul did not place a premium on ignorance, nor in the least respect disparage a thorough education. He did not regard his learning as worthless. But he understood what so few realize today, that education sought and acquired for a purely selfish purpose is idolatry. He conceived the value of education to lie in the ability it imparted to comprehend more fully and teach more effectively the gospel of the crucified Christ. He implies that learning is not to be sought as an end in itself, but as a means to the exalted end of revealing and glorifying the Saviour of the world.

This purpose of Paul, so faithfully pursued, explains the profound and lasting influence and the mighty achievements of his life. He did not fully realize, at the beginning of his ministry, that the preaching of the cross was, above all else, the power of God. Not without some bitter experience did he learn this truth. This is evident from the historic account of his visit to the cultured city of Athens.

"As Paul journeyed from Berea, he stopped at Athens to await the arrival of Silas and Timotheus; and 'his spirit was stirred in him, when he saw the city wholly given to idolatry. Therefore disputed he in the synagogue with the Jews, and with the devout persons, and in the market daily with them that met with him. Then certain philosophers of the Epicureans, and of the Stoics, encountered him. And some said, What will this babbler say? other some, He seemeth to be a setter forth of strange gods: because he preached unto them Jesus, and the resurrection.'

"The philosophers who entered into conversation with the apostle were soon convinced that his knowledge exceeded their own. He was competent to meet their opposition on their own ground, matching logic with logic, learning with learning, philosophy with philosophy, and oratory with oratory.

"At the close of his labors he looked for the results of his work. Out of the large assembly that had listened to his eloquent words, only three had been converted to the faith. He then decided that from that time he would maintain the simplicity of the gospel.

He was convinced that the learning of the world was powerless to move the hearts of men, but that the gospel was the power of God unto salvation."

It is Christ crucified that appeals to the hearts of men, weakened and enslaved by sin. Many things appeal to the intellect, but if the heart is not touched and moved till the will is surrendered to Christ, it avails nothing.

Paul declared that all he had learned or achieved was of value only so far as it could be used to reveal Christ crucified. All that could not be so used was cast aside as worthless. "What things were gain to me, those I counted loss for Christ. Yea doubtless, and I count all things but loss for the excellency of the knowledge of Christ Jesus my Lord: for whom I have suffered the loss of all things, and do count them but dung, that I may win Christ."

Paul was not a preacher of mere creeds or theories. Christ crucified was the supreme object and theme of his ministry. *To a great extent the Christian world today has lost this emphasis on the cross.* The church is comparatively weak, not because the gospel has lost its power, but because something else has been substituted for the preaching of the cross. Should Christians live in the atmosphere of the cross today as the early disciples did, they would have a much deeper spiritual experience individually, and this would make it possible for the mighty working of the Spirit as in apostolic days.

In what sublime, yet simple words the Saviour summed up the everlasting gospel. "God so loved the world, that He gave His only-begotten Son, that whosoever believeth in Him should not perish, but have everlasting life." It is the Son of God uplifted on the cross as man's substitute, that arrests the attention and awakens the interest of sinners. Christ exalted in heaven may not appeal to them, but Christ suffering and dying under the curse of sin, and in the sinner's stead, finds a response.

Degraded and enslaved by evil practices, the sinner feels only fear and aversion toward God; but a look at Calvary reveals the truth that God loves sinners. Through all the ages the reverent presentation of the Christ of Calvary has touched and melted hearts. We cannot place too much emphasis upon this, the central truth of Christianity; for on the cross our every hope depends, and in its light alone is the way of salvation made plain.

Today God is sending His final message of mercy to the world. The prophecies clearly teach that the promise of Christ to return and gather His believing children out of the unbelieving world to the heavenly mansions He has prepared, will be fulfilled in this generation. Men and women who are under condemnation of the divine law for their past sins, and are still enslaved by evil habits and practices, are unfit for the presence of God, and could not possibly expect to be welcomed into heaven. A great work of preparation is necessary. God has provided that poor sinners may be justified, cleansed, and sanctified so that they reflect the image and character of Christ, and thus be fitted to dwell with Him above. The fulfillment of prophecy emphasizing the final solemn call of God to man is designed to arouse the people, awaken conviction, and lead them to seek repentance and the preparation necessary to fit them for translation to heaven.

But what shall they do when they are aroused? What ought men to do when they are awakened by the most convincing evidence from God to realize that they are living very near the close of time? There is one supreme and all-important thing to do, and that is to focus their attention on the cross of Christ. That is the source of their salvation. They must be pardoned, cleansed, transformed, victorious. This cannot be brought about by any creed or dogma, system or theory, new or old. "There is none other name under heaven . . . whereby we must be saved," but the name of Jesus. Salvation is not the result of adopting a creed, embracing a doctrine, or believing a theory, but of receiving a *person*. "As many as *received Him,* to them gave He power to become the sons of God."

The chief reason why thousands of Christians find little peace and satisfaction and contentment in the Christian experience, lies in their failure to grasp this great truth. The record of their spiritual life is largely one of oft-repeated struggle and resolution ending in failure and defeat. They long for an experience that will bring them satisfaction and joy, peace and victory. They believe the great doctrines of the Bible, and accept them all as the word of God. They pray, and study, and attend church services, and perform definite work for Christ. They go through all the forms of Christian activity that are designed to help in attaining and perfecting Christian character, but all the time they are conscious that something vital is lacking. Let me give a homely illustration to show how many Christians there are to whom the personal presence of Christ is not a reality.

I have a friend whom I urge to come to my home and make an extended visit. An unexpected opportunity arises, and some morning he knocks at my door. I welcome him, telling him how delighted I am, and eagerly urge him to remain as long as possible. I take his hat and coat, show him to a seat, and then, excusing myself, I retire to another room. He waits, expecting me to return in a moment, but an hour passes, and he is still alone. He looks over papers and books and pictures, waiting patiently hour after hour, but anxiously wondering what could have occurred to delay me so long. He cannot believe that I have wholly forgotten him, nor that I merely pretended to desire his presence. All day he remains alone while I busy myself about other matters. Surely one would never treat a friend so unkindly and discourteously, and yet hundreds of Christians have admitted to me that this is the way they treat the Saviour. They speak to Him a moment in the morning, inviting Him into their hearts and asking Him to bless and keep them, and they go about their own affairs, never even giving Him another thought till night.

Surely such people have not "received Him;" they have only accepted a theory. If we do not know Jesus Christ as a real living, loving, divine Person, coming into our hearts in the morning, and if we do not talk with Him and listen as He speaks to us, then we shall not be satisfied, but shall ever be conscious of a lack. For the power that is needed to transform our lives and give victory moment by moment is not in a doctrine, but in this Person.

The reality of the presence of Christ to each believer can be understood only in the light of the cross. This is why the apostle Paul placed the supreme emphasis on Christ crucified, and ever sought to focus the gaze of men on Him. In all the history of God's work through men, those who achieved the greatest success were those to whom the presence of Christ was most real. What could be more important and more reasonable than for every person who professes to believe in Christ and depend upon Him for present and eternal salvation, to cultivate that constant fellowship with Him that will make His presence a great reality?

"As the mind dwells upon Christ, the character is molded after the divine similitude. The thoughts are pervaded with a sense of His goodness, His love. We contemplate His character, and thus He is in all our thoughts. His love encloses us. If we gaze even a moment upon the sun in its meridian glory, when we turn away our eyes, the image of the sun will appear in everything upon which we look. Thus it is when we behold Jesus; everything we look upon reflects His image, the Sun of Righteousness. We cannot see anything else or talk of anything else. His image is imprinted upon the eye of the soul, and affects every portion of our daily life, softening and subduing our whole nature."—*"Testimonies to Ministers," pp. 388, 389.*

It is singular that so many people say they are unable to make Christ seem real. Millions of people seem to have no difficulty in making things seem real which do not exist and are utterly absurd; while here is the supreme fundamental fact upon which the eternal hope of every human being rests, and which is attested by the infallible word of God, and men say, It does not seem real.

We should not overlook the fact that the friendship of Jesus must be cultivated the same as that of any other friend. People are most real to us whom we love the most, think of the most, and whose presence we seek the most. When the mind is occupied nearly all the time with secular thoughts to the exclusion of Christ, it is inconsistent to expect that His presence will ever become real. We cannot think secular thoughts, study secular books, perform secular work, or engage in secular conversation fifteen hours out of sixteen, and expect to become spiritually minded. And unless we are spiritual, we cannot have fellowship with Christ, and be deeply conscious of the reality of His presence. This does not mean that we must lay aside schoolbooks, or manual labor, or conversation concerning business, all of which are regarded as secular. But it is possible to sustain such a close relationship to Christ that our whole being will be spiritualized, and the atmosphere of His presence will pervade all the ordinary, necessary duties of life.

What a marvelous change would take place in the lives of professed Christians if they would keep fresh in memory the scenes of Calvary! How much that is cheap and common and superficial would be replaced by that which is pure and noble and exalted, which would attract men and women to Christ!

The early disciples well understood that it was the preaching of Christ crucified that gripped the hearts of men. It is not the preaching of the historic Christ who lived two thousand years ago that appeals primarily to lost men and women. It is not Christ sitting at the right hand of the Father, reigning in glory. It is the Christ of the cross.

A man lost in the depths of discouragement and despair because of his failure to reach his ideals of purity and nobility and right, looks up at Christ in glory, and sees only an impassable gulf. But if he can be induced to look at Christ hanging on the cross as his substitute, wounded for his transgressions, bruised for his iniquities, bearing his sins in His own body on the tree, that he may be pardoned and saved, he can hardly resist such an appeal. It leads him to the foot of the cross in penitence and faith.

> "If the wanderer his mistake discern,
> Judge his own way, and sigh for a return,
> Bewildered once, must he bewail his loss
> Forever and forever? No—the cross!
> There, and there only, is the power to save.
> There no delusive hope invites despair;
> No mockery meets you, no delusion there;
> The spell and charms that blinded you before,
> All vanish there, and fascinate no more."

It is doubtless the enemy's studied purpose to induce religious teachers and preachers to introduce many themes to supplant and supplement the preaching of the cross. The present-day lack of power to win souls indicates the measure of his success. Today, as in the days of Paul, the preaching of Christ crucified is "the power of God, and the wisdom of God."

"If those who today are teaching the word of God, would uplift the cross of Christ higher and still higher, their ministry would be far more successful. If sinners can be led to give one earnest look at the cross, if they can obtain a full view of the crucified Saviour, they will realize the depth of God's compassion and the sinfulness of sin."—*"The Acts of the Apostles,"* page 209.

37

"Bring the thrilling scene
Home to my inmost soul; the Sufferer's cry,
'Father, if it be possible, this cup
Take Thou away, yet not My will, but Thine;'
The sleeping friends who could not watch one hour;
The torch, the flashing sword, the traitor's kiss;
The astonished angel, with the tear of heaven
Upon his cheek, still striving to assuage
Those fearful pangs that bowed the Son of God
Like a bruisèd reed."

Some time ago I witnessed a striking illustration of
the mighty and immediate result of uplifting the crucified Saviour. I was speaking to a large congregation on
the subject of the cross. All appeared deeply interested, and were giving the closest attention, with the
exception of one young lady, who sat in the corner at
the rear of the room. She was whispering to those
about her, preventing their listening and creating
some disturbance. I stopped a moment, and, gaining
their attention, I related an incident which set forth
briefly but sympathetically the sacrifice of Christ on
the cross to save sinners. All were very quiet, and at
the close of the meeting I invited any who desired to
turn to Christ or seek spiritual help to remain for the
aftermeeting.

A large number remained, and soon young men and
women were confessing their sins and surrendering
their lives to the Saviour. Presently the young lady
who had been whispering arose and said, "I have
never before been interested in religion or cared to
be a Christian. But tonight when I saw so vividly the
Saviour dying on the cross for my sins, it broke my
hard heart, and I now give my life wholly to Him."

GETHSEMANE

In the consideration of the cross as it represents the atoning sacrifice of Christ, it is well to begin with the experiences of Gethsemane.

> "Wouldst thou learn the depths of sin,
>   All its bitterness and pain;
> What it cost thy God to win
>   Sinners to Himself again?
> Come, poor sinner, come with me;
>   Visit sad Gethsemane."

"He came out, and went, as He was wont, to the Mount of Olives; and His disciples also followed Him. And when He was at the place, He said unto them, Pray that ye enter not into temptation. And He was withdrawn from them about a stone's cast, and kneeled down; and prayed, saying, Father, if Thou be willing, remove this cup from Me: nevertheless not My will, but Thine be done. . . . And being in an agony He prayed more earnestly: and His sweat was as it were great drops of blood falling down to the ground." Luke 22:39-44.

Each step of the way, from His humble birth in Bethlehem to this hour, Jesus had chosen for Himself and had taken every step voluntarily. He offered Himself to God to be the propitiation for man's sins, and now He proposed to complete the work by drinking the last bitter cup. He sought the solitude of Gethsemane, there to enter that dark valley which would end in the sinner's death.

Jesus had spent many nights in prayer and communion with His Father, but never before such a night as this. It was not for deliverance from physical suffering, nor from the hands of His persecutors, nor from the shame and ignominy of public execution, nor from the cruel death of the cross, that He prayed. All these He had foreseen and willingly chosen as part of the price of our redemption. He did not seek to escape the inevitable and necessary consequences of taking the sinner's place.

That from which He prayed to be delivered was infinitely more dreadful than mortal death. The penalty for sin is exclusion from the presence of God, and this, as our substitute, Jesus must suffer. Nevertheless it was proper and becoming that He should wish this last and bitterest sorrow might be shortened or removed. How could the celestial beings who were looking on have understood the horror of sin, and the inconceivable cost of redemption, had He faced the hour of abandonment and despair in the outer darkness of spiritual separation from the Father as the representative sinner, with no uttered cry of anguish, no protest or appeal? Throughout His whole life Jesus was consumed with the supreme desire to please and honor and glorify His Father. He was constantly occupied with His Father's work, speaking His Father's words, and seeking to advance His Father's interests. Now a black, impenetrable wall of sin was about to separate them. Though He and His Father were perfectly agreed in paying this awful price for the redemption of the lost race, yet it was most becoming for Jesus, in the presence of the onlooking universe, to cry out against an experience so dreadful.

How this very prayer to have the cup removed must have endeared Him to the Father, since it expressed a love which ignored all the indescribable sorrow which men and demons imposed, regarding them as utterly insignificant compared with the overwhelming anguish of the withdrawal of the Father's loving presence and approval.

The law demanded the death of the sinner. Jesus understood the requirements of justice, and willingly offered Himself as the victim. The shame and disgrace of the crucifixion, the anguish of the physical suffering, the assaults of the hosts of demons, and the curse of the violated law,—all these He faced. But must He actually be excluded from the presence of His own dear Father? Must He endure all this in that outer darkness of spiritual separation and God abandonment, where "there is weeping and gnashing of teeth"?

As He entered the dark shadows of Gethsemane, the realization of that mysterious curse of sin was so much more dreadful than its anticipation that the disciple testified, He "began to be sore amazed, and to be very heavy." He longed for sympathy and comfort from His followers, but how little they understood the pathetic appeal, "My soul is exceeding sorrowful, even unto death."

The awful burden of a world's guilt began to settle down upon His soul, shutting out the light and peace of His Father's presence. By actual experience He was beginning to "taste death for every man."

"As the Son of God bowed in the attitude of prayer in the garden of Gethsemane, the agony of His spirit forced from His pores sweat like great drops of blood. It was here that the horror of great darkness surrounded Him. The sins of the world were upon Him. He was suffering in man's stead, as a transgressor of His Father's law. Here was the scene of temptation. The divine light of God was receding from His vision, and He was passing into the hands of the powers of darkness. In His soul anguish He lay prostrate on the cold earth. He was realizing His Father's frown. He had taken the cup of suffering from the lips of guilty man, and proposed to drink it Himself, and in its place give to man the cup of blessing. The wrath that would have fallen upon man, was now falling upon Christ. It was here that the mysterious cup trembled in His hand. . . .

"Leaving His disciples within hearing of His voice, He went a little distance from them, and fell on His face, and prayed. His soul was agonized, and He pleaded, 'O My Father, if it be possible, let this cup pass from Me; nevertheless, not as I will, but as Thou wilt.' The sins of a lost world were upon Him, and overwhelming Him. It was a sense of His Father's frown, in consequence of sin, which rent His heart with such piercing agony, and forced from His brow great drops of blood, which, rolling down His pale cheeks, fell to the ground, moistening the earth."— *"Testimonies for the Church," Vol. II, pp. 203, 204.*

Why did Jesus shrink from the ordeal, instead of facing death like the heroic martyrs? The answer is that the martyrs were facing mere mortal death, and were sustained in their sufferings by the consciousness of God's presence and acceptance. But Christ was taking the sinner's place, and as the typical, representative sinner He was bearing our load of guilt out into the darkness of separation from God. As the sins of the world engulfed Him like a vast ocean, He felt Himself sinking into a darkness He had never before known. It seemed more than His human body could sustain, and immediate death threatened Him. But how then could His own predictions concerning Himself be fulfilled?

Though He might have laid down His life in the garden, and the sacrifice have been acceptable to the Father, yet how difficult it would have been for men to understand and appropriate what He had done. There is a moral shock connected with the awful tragedy of the crucifixion, which the Spirit of God uses to stir the consciences of men, arousing their moral sensibilities, and awakening them from their stupor and blindness and selfishness.

How long was the Saviour engaged in this mighty struggle in Gethsemane? He had been with the disciples at the Passover supper, and they had sung a hymn and started for the garden. It could not have taken long to walk to the familiar place. So it would appear that Jesus spent several hours in supplication.

As He wrestled earnestly in prayer and the burden seemed to grow heavier, rather than lighter, He arose and sought the disciples. Finding them asleep, He returned and fell upon His face, repeating the sorrowful words. The weight of the darkness and curse seemed more than He could endure, and again He came to the disciples. Receiving no human sympathy or encouragement, He returned the second time. The sorrow and anguish of those long hours, into which "eternities were compressed," we shall never be able fully to comprehend. His suffering was so intense that it seemed to dry up the very springs of thought and narrow the words of prayer down to the one intense, burning appeal. Doubtless in short ejaculations the words were repeated again and again as the hours dragged slowly by, "O My Father, My Father—if it be possible—all things are possible with Thee: if it be possible—Father—this cup—let it pass: nevertheless, Father, not My will—but Thine—be done."

"The moon was shining yet. The orient's brow,
Set with the morning star, was not yet dim;
And the deep silence which subdues the breath
Like a strong feeling, hung upon the world
As sleep upon the pulses of a child.
'Twas the last watch of night. Gethsemane,
With its bathed leaves of silver, seemed dissolved
In visible stillness; and as Jesus' voice,
With its bewildering sweetness, met the ear
Of His disciples, it vibrated on
Like the first whisper in a silent world.
They came on slowly. Heaviness oppressed
The Saviour's heart, and when the kindness
Of His deep love was poured, He felt the need
Of near communion, for His gift of strength
Was wasted by the spirit's weariness.
He left them there, and went a little on,
And in the depth of that hushed silentness,
Alone with God, He fell upon His face,

43

> And as His heart was broken with the rush
> Of His surpassing agony, and death
> Wrung to Him from a dying universe,
> Was mightier than the Son of man could bear,
> He gave His sorrows way, and in the deep
> Prostration of His soul, breathed out the prayer."

During all those hours, as He lay prostrate on the ground, looking forward with indescribable anguish to the time when the curse of God should fall with full weight upon Him, the one thing which seemed too terrible to endure He never once named. The reality was so much more dreadful than the anticipation, that He could not bring Himself to frame the words. The agony, so intense that great drops of bloody sweat fell from His face, never wrung it from His lips. He called it "the cup." "O My Father, let this cup pass." Only once, at the last, at the very end, from the midst of the appalling darkness of Calvary, with a piercing cry it burst from His lips.

Christ prayed that His Father's will should be done, and it was not the Father's will that He should die there in the garden. Divine help came, for "there appeared an angel unto Him from heaven, strengthening Him." It is written of Jesus that "in the days of His flesh" He "offered up prayers and supplications with strong crying and tears unto Him that was able to save Him from death, and was heard in that He feared." Jesus did not ask to be saved from dying, but He did pray most earnestly to be saved from death. In order to redeem the lost, it was necessary that He should die in the sinner's place and as his substitute, and this Jesus voluntarily offered to do, and for that purpose He came into the world. But the appalling temptation pressing upon His heart as He went out into the darkness, was that "sin was so offensive in the sight of His Father that He could not be reconciled to His Son." This Jesus prayed against with all the intensity of His divine-human soul, and His prayer prevailed. He died, and He was saved from death.

44

CALVARY

Our appreciation of the redemption wrought for us by the Saviour on the cross will be in proportion to our realization of that from which we are rescued. Being saved from sin, we are also saved from the wages of sin. The Scripture says, "The soul that sinneth, it shall die," and, "The wages of sin is death."

What is this death which is the wages of sin, and which Christ must have suffered as our substitute? It is evident that many regard the penalty for sin lightly. We read in the daily paper of some notorious criminal who has been tried and sentenced to death. Every detail of his conduct is graphically described. He appears utterly hardened and stoical. He marches unmoved to the place of execution, and to the last moment exhibits no sign of fear or dread. To many this hardened stoicism appears quite heroic, and seems to form the basis of their conception of the proper attitude of one who rejects God's mercy, and expects to receive the final punishment for his sins. Of course that is a very superficial view, but there is much that is superficial today in religion, as in other things.

There are two methods which the enemy constantly employs to involve men in spiritual ruin. He endeavors to make them disbelieve God's word. Failing in this, he seeks to introduce into their minds a false or perverted theory of the word. One method may be as successful, and the result as disastrous, as the other. One man claims to disbelieve in hell altogether; another believes in an eternally burning, torturing hell.

These theories are utterly at variance with the teaching of the Scriptures concerning the wages of sin, and also with the character of a God who is both infinitely merciful and infinitely just. Much of the emphasis is placed on the physical aspect of the punishment for sin, whereas sin is a moral and spiritual matter, and therefore the penalty must be visited chiefly in that realm.

Civil governments inflict the penalty of physical death for the violation of certain civil laws, but it cannot be supposed that the Ruler of the universe would impose no severer punishment for the transgression of an infinitely holy, perfect, unchangeable, and necessary moral law. God gave this law to safeguard the highest interests of all created beings. It is the law of love. If obeyed, it results in eternal life, peace, and happiness. If disobeyed, it must bring a punishment proportionate to the infinite blessings rewarding obedience. This punishment is inconceivably terrible, and to ascertain what it is, and learn all that the Scriptures reveal concerning it, is the duty of every rational being. If we choose to obey God, and thus escape the penalty of sin, we need to be intelligent concerning that penalty, that we may adequately appreciate the mercy and love of God. If we do not choose to accept salvation, we would be most irrational to plunge headlong into an eternity of which we know nothing.

Surely no intelligent, candid person can study the Scriptures and fail to understand that those who persistently refuse to accept God's plan of salvation as revealed in His word, inevitably bring upon themselves a fearful doom. The Bible leaves no room for uncertainty in this matter.

"These shall go away into everlasting punishment: but the righteous into life eternal." Matt. 25:46.

"Ye serpents, ye generation of vipers, how can ye escape the damnation of hell?" Matt. 23:33.

"Many of them that sleep in the dust of the earth

46

shall awake, some to everlasting life, and some to shame and everlasting contempt." Dan. 12:2.

"Who shall be punished with everlasting destruction from the presence of the Lord, and from the glory of His power." 2 Thess. 1:9.

The penalty is just and necessary. God would cease to be a moral being if He maintained immoral beings in union with Himself. At the time of the great rebellion in heaven, God was charged with being unjust and arbitrary in His requirements. God maintained that His law was a law of love, and was just and necessary. Should any intelligent being now disobey God, and the penalty be set aside, it would be an admission on the part of God before the whole universe that the charge against Him was true, that His law was either unjust or unnecessary. Therefore, God must visit the penalty upon every transgressor, in order to vindicate the righteousness of His own government. And if He in any case remits the penalty, He must first devise some means of justifying His course before the universe, and demonstrating His righteousness in so doing.

So God instituted the great plan of redemption by substitution. If the sinner does not suffer the wages of his sins, it must be because someone else, acceptable to God, has suffered the penalty for him. God's love for man was so great that He Himself provided a substitute in the person of His Son. This is the gospel. "God so loved the world, that He gave His only-begotten Son, that whosoever believeth in Him should not perish, but have everlasting life."

All men are sinners. "The wages of sin is death." Pardon and restoration to holiness and divine favor can come only through God's acceptance of the death of an innocent substitute for the guilty sinner. The whole sacrificial system practiced so many centuries by God's people, was designed to keep this great truth constantly before them.

A sinner could, by his own death, meet the demands

47

of the broken law, but no sinner could atone for the transgressions of another. Even had there been one sinless man on earth, his death could have been accepted for but one sinner. Furthermore, since mere physical death could not atone for the spiritual death entailed by sin, the innocent substitute must have been eternally lost. Nothing would be gained by permitting a righteous man to be eternally lost in order that an unrighteous man might be saved. But the Creator, unwilling that man should perish in his sins, provided a Substitute capable of redeeming the whole race. This is the gospel which in all ages God has been revealing to man. There is no escape for any human being who has violated the divine law, except the one avenue which God in infinite love and mercy devised to save sinners.

"How much more shall the blood of Christ, who through the eternal Spirit offered Himself without spot to God, purge your conscience from dead works to serve the living God?"

Jesus Christ "offered Himself" to God to take the sinner's place. By this course He would vindicate the law of God, proving that it is infinitely holy, just, and good, and at the same time make it possible for God to extend mercy to the penitent sinner. Christ understood that He would be required to suffer the exact penalty the worst sinner deserved. God said, "The soul that sinneth, it shall die;" therefore, Jesus Christ must die as the sinner would have died. This the Saviour volunteered to do. If we would appreciate what we are saved from, if we would have some adequate realization of what the finally impenitent must meet, we should study the death that Jesus died.

Again we ask, What is that death which is the wages of sin, and which every human being will suffer or escape according to his own choice? Only one Man has ever lived in this world who has suffered that death, and who is thereby qualified to give us information concerning it.

"We see Jesus, who was made a little lower than the angels for the suffering of death, crowned with glory and honor; that He by the grace of God should taste death for every man." Heb. 2:9.

Knowing by experience the indescribable horror of the sinner's fate, Christ has given us some very solemn warnings concerning it:

"I say unto you, That many shall come from the east and west, and shall sit down with Abraham, and Isaac, and Jacob, in the kingdom of heaven. But the children of the kingdom *shall be cast out into outer darkness: there shall be weeping and gnashing of teeth.*" Matt. 8:11, 12.

"When the king came in to see the guests, he saw there a man which had not on a wedding garment: and he saith unto him, Friend, how camest thou in hither not having a wedding garment? And he was speechless. Then said the king to the servants, Bind him hand and foot, and take him away, and *cast him into outer darkness; there shall be weeping and gnashing of teeth.*" Matt. 22:11-13.

"But and if that evil servant shall say in his heart, My lord delayeth his coming, . . . the lord of that servant shall come in a day when he looketh not for him, and in an hour that he is not aware of, and shall cut him asunder, and appoint him his portion with the hypocrites: *there shall be weeping and gnashing of teeth.*" Matt. 24:48-51.

"Take therefore the talent from him, and give it unto him which hath ten talents. . . . And *cast ye the unprofitable servant into outer darkness: there shall be weeping and gnashing of teeth.*" Matt. 25: 28-30.

"Then said one unto Him, Lord, are there few that be saved? And He said unto them, Strive to enter in at the strait gate: for many, I say unto you, will seek to enter in, and shall not be able." *"There shall be weeping and gnashing of teeth,* when ye shall see Abraham, and Isaac, and Jacob, and all the prophets,

in the kingdom of God, and *you yourselves thrust out.*"
Luke 13:23, 28.

Probably the most dreadful punishment men can inflict is solitary confinement in darkness. It often drives men insane.

God has attached to the violation of His law a penalty that is just and necessary. It is eternal exclusion and banishment from His presence. It is the "outer darkness," where there is "weeping and gnashing of teeth." Eventually the result, or consequence, of this separation from God will be physical death. This is set forth in two other statements by Christ:

"The Son of man shall send forth His angels, and they shall gather out of His kingdom all things that offend, and them which do iniquity; and shall cast them into a furnace of fire: there shall be wailing and gnashing of teeth." Matt. 13:41, 42.

"Whose fan is in His hand, and He will thoroughly purge His floor, and gather His wheat into the garner; but He will burn up the chaff with unquenchable fire." Matt. 3:12.

When those who have determinedly and persistently refused all God's offers of mercy and pardon, have received the just wages of their own obstinate choice, they will be cast "into a furnace of fire," and burned up as chaff. But let no one think that the awful penalty which Christ endured as our substitute, and which the finally impenitent must endure, is a light matter.

When Jesus arrived at Golgotha, He was nailed to the cross, and it was uplifted and thrust into the place prepared for it. That mysterious transaction between God and His Son which was about to take place, marked the farthest point to which it was necessary to go to save sinners. There alone the Saviour could achieve that union with fallen men which was necessary to become their Substitute and Redeemer. The sufferings of the Deity did not begin nor end at the cross, but they focused there; hence the crucifixion marks the supreme moment, or climax, of the plan of redemption.

The prophecies concerning the death of God's Son were about fulfilled. Around the cross thronged a vast multitude. As the nails were driven into His hands, He prayed, "Father, forgive them; for they know not what they do." How true it was! they knew not what they did, nor what He was doing. While they were crucifying Him, He was redeeming them, and they sensed it not. The crowd saw only a human tragedy, and supposed this to be the end of one whose claim to heavenly origin was apparently coming to nought.

The sins of the world were now resting upon Jesus. Did you ever stop to think how it would look could you see a scroll large enough to have written upon it all the sins that have been committed by human beings in six thousand years? What an appalling record! How it staggers the mind to contemplate it! Had these sins all been written out and placed in the hands of Jesus, the burden could not have been more real than it was at that hour. In Gethsemane, Christ had experienced a foretaste of the anguish of that moment when He, as the sinner's substitute, should descend into the outer darkness of spiritual separation from God. This penalty is something far beyond the possibility of man to inflict.

"Upon Christ as our substitute and surety was laid the iniquity of us all. He was counted a transgressor, that He might redeem us from the condemnation of the law. The guilt of every descendant of Adam was pressing upon His heart. The wrath of God against sin, the terrible manifestation of His displeasure because of iniquity, filled the soul of His Son with consternation. All His life Christ had been publishing to a fallen world the good news of the Father's mercy and pardoning love. Salvation for the chief of sinners was His theme. But now with the terrible weight of

51

guilt He bears, He cannot see the Father's reconciling face. The withdrawal of the divine countenance from the Saviour in this hour of supreme anguish pierced His heart with a sorrow that can never be fully understood by man. So great was this agony that His physical pain was hardly felt.

"Satan with his fierce temptations wrung the heart of Jesus. The Saviour could not see through the portals of the tomb. Hope did not present to Him His coming forth from the grave a conqueror, or tell Him of the Father's acceptance of the sacrifice. He feared that sin was so offensive to God, that their separation was to be eternal. Christ felt the anguish which the sinner will feel when mercy shall no longer plead for the guilty race. It was the sense of sin, bringing the Father's wrath upon Him as man's substitute, that made the cup He drank so bitter, and broke the heart of the Son of God."—*"The Desire of Ages," pp. 752, 753.*

There is much about the matchless love of God in the gift of His Son to our fallen world that is mysterious and beyond the comprehension of our finite minds. The amazing condescension of Christ in uniting His divinity with our poor fallen humanity, is difficult to grasp.

But as we contemplate this moment of supreme crisis on the cross, the mind fairly staggers in its effort to appreciate such unfathomable love. Jesus Christ, with all the weight of the world's sins upon Him, was facing that outer darkness of spiritual separation from His Father, a region as yet unexplored by any human being. Demons with all their satanic ingenuity were seeking to deepen the darkness about His soul. And the awful temptation was tugging at His heart that sin was so offensive in the sight of His Father that He could not be reconciled to His Son, that He was descending into a darkness that would be eternal. Even then He might have come down from the cross and refused to drink the cup, but, oh, amazing love!

He determined to open the way to eternal joy for us, at any cost to Himself. Well may we join the devout poet in singing:

> "When I survey the wondrous cross
>   On which the Prince of Glory died,
> My richest gain I count but loss,
>   And pour contempt on all my pride."

For three long hours the earth was covered with a dense pall of darkness. Vivid flashes of lightning centering upon the cross seemed like the thunderbolts of divine wrath aimed at the dying Sufferer. During those three hours no words had escaped His lips. "As a sheep before her shearers is dumb, so He openeth not His mouth." The consciousness of His Father's presence which had sustained Him throughout His life, had left Him. He was drinking that dreadful cup over which He had wrestled so many hours in Gethsemane, but which He had never named. But now, with a sudden cry of inexpressible woe, the words burst from His lips, "My God, My God, why hast Thou forsaken Me?"

He did not cry, "My Father," for He was grappling with the overwhelming sense of abandonment and despair. All the pain and agony and torture of the crucifixion were as nothing to the horror of spiritual separation from God. In descending into that outer darkness He was suffering not only the sorrows of death, but the pains of hell.

"The sorrows of death compassed Me, and the pains of hell gat hold upon Me." "Great is Thy mercy toward Me: and Thou hast delivered My soul from the lowest hell."

Think of it, sinner! all this was endured by thy Redeemer to rescue thee from eternal death, and open the gates for thee into eternal bliss and glory. How canst thou despise and reject such a Saviour? How canst thou turn from such a loving and reasonable appeal?

"I gave My life for thee,
 My precious blood I shed,
That thou might'st ransomed be,
 And quickened from the dead;
I gave, I gave My life for thee,
What hast thou given for Me?

"I suffered much for thee,
 More than thy tongue can tell,
Of bit'rest agony,
 To rescue thee from hell;
I've borne, I've borne it all for thee,
What hast thou borne for Me?"

"When Jesus therefore had received the vinegar, He said, *It is finished.*" When that cry rang out in "clear, trumpetlike tones that seemed to resound throughout creation," it marked the most sublime moment of all time for the human race. The great sacrifice was made, and salvation was assured to all who would accept. He had gone down in the sinner's place. He had shed His blood and paid the debt.

The Saviour descended to this awful extremity of suffering for sin, that He might bring us to God. When the requirements of divine justice were fully met and the sacrifice complete, He declared, "It is finished." He had given all that infinite love could give. There was a moment of exultant joy that the task was completed and that eternal redemption for sinners was secure. Then the last cry of "Father," this time a cry of perfect resignation and trust, "into Thy hands I commend My spirit: and having said thus, He gave up the ghost."

As soon as He had fully carried out the terms of the covenant entered into between Himself and the Father, He surrendered up His physical life. He tasted death for every man. He had exalted the divine law, and shown its eternal and immutable character. He had vindicated the justice and love of God by the shedding of His own blood for man's redemption.

But since it is declared that the wages of sin is death—spiritual separation from God and destruction from His presence—some do not understand how He could have suffered so great a penalty in so brief a time. Doubtless there is much in the atonement which we can neither explain nor comprehend. We know that His human capacity for suffering must have exceeded all our understanding. In all His life not one spot or stain of sin had ever tarnished His mind. Not once did He diverge from the path of purity and obedience. His physical senses were never weakened and benumbed by the indulgence of depraved appetite or debasing practices. The exquisite sensitiveness of His perfect being would give Him a capacity for suffering immeasurably beyond that of the sinner.

But above all this we must consider the participation of the Deity in the offering for sin. Jesus was not only the Son of man, but He was the Son of God. Leaving the glories of that upper world in which He was worshiped and adored as Creator and King, He descended to this fallen world, and "made Himself of no reputation, and took upon Him the form of a servant, and was made in the likeness of men: and being found in fashion as a man, He humbled Himself, and became obedient unto death, even the death of the cross." Phil. 2:7, 8.

Nothing less than the sacrifice of the Son of God as well as the Son of man was sufficient for the ransom of one soul. Nothing more than that is required for the redemption of every member of the human race. The great plan of the ages has now been carried out. "Those things which God before had showed by the mouth of all His prophets, that Christ should suffer, He hath so fulfilled." Acts 3:18.

"Through all depths of sin and loss,
Drop the plummet of the cross;
Never yet abyss was found,
Deeper than the cross could sound."

"Though now He has ascended to the presence of God, and shares the throne of the universe, Jesus has lost none of His compassionate nature. Today the same tender, sympathizing heart is open to all the woes of humanity. Today the hand that was pierced is reached forth to bless more abundantly His people that are in the world. . . . The soul that has given himself to Christ is more precious in His sight than the whole world. The Saviour would have passed through the agony of Calvary, that one might be saved in His kingdom. He will never abandon one for whom He has died."—*"The Desire of Ages," p. 480.*

> "And hast thou heard, and hast not heeded yet?
> Then turn, in heaven's name, and take the hand,
> Nail pierced for you, that stretches out in love
> To give you gifts more precious than the wealth
> Of all earth's millions blended into one.
> Oh, grasp that hand, and know the blessed joy
> Of sins forgiven, and the comfort of
> His all-abounding grace that heals the wounds
> Of sin, and every sadness mollifies.
> Thy Saviour waits, and shall He wait in vain?"

Sin means eternal separation from God. It means the outer darkness of abandonment and despair, where there is weeping and gnashing of teeth. It means eternal exclusion from the glory and joy of the children of God.

But the cross means reconciliation and union with the heavenly Father. It means an eternity of life and peace and happiness—eternal fellowship with the King of kings, who humbled Himself to become our brother and to die for our salvation. Each individual decides his eternal destiny by his own choice and by his attitude toward the cross of Christ. How irrational that any intelligent human being should close his eyes to this stupendous fact!

THE VICTORY OF THE CROSS

The magnetism of the cross draws us back again and again to contemplate its mysteries and to rejoice in its triumphs. Thus it was with the men of God of ancient times, to whom the great salvation was a matter of prophecy and promise, prefigured by sacrificial types and offerings. "Of which salvation the prophets have inquired and searched diligently, who prophesied of the grace that should come unto you: searching what, or what manner of time the Spirit of Christ which was in them did signify, when it testified beforehand the sufferings of Christ, and the glory that should follow." 1 Peter 1:10, 11.

Many of the prophecies must have been mysterious and baffling even to the men through whom they were given. The promise to Abraham of a Redeemer indicated that He was to become one of our race. "In thy seed shall all the nations of the earth be blessed." Another prophecy foretells in Him the union of divinity with humanity: "Therefore the Lord Himself shall give you a sign: Behold, a virgin shall conceive, and bear a son, and shall call His name Emmanuel"—God with us. "Unto us a child is born, unto us a son is given: and the government shall be upon His shoulder: and His name shall be called Wonderful, Counselor, The mighty God, The everlasting Father, The Prince of Peace."

But most strange and startling and incomprehensible were those prophecies which testified beforehand of the sufferings of the Messiah. There are two special chapters in the Old Testament devoted wholly to a description of the sufferings of Christ. The fifty-third chapter of Isaiah describes vividly and in detail the mission of Jesus as He offered Himself to be man's substitute, taking the sinner's burden of guilt, and receiving his punishment. It is impressive to go through the chapter carefully, and note each statement which sets forth His vicarious suffering to atone for the sins of men.

"Surely He hath borne our griefs,
  And carried our sorrows."
"He was wounded for our transgressions,
  He was bruised for our iniquities:
  The chastisement of our peace was upon Him;
  And with His stripes we are healed."
"The Lord hath laid on Him the iniquity of us all."
"For the transgression of my people was He stricken.
  And He made His grave with the wicked,
  And with the rich in His death."
"By His knowledge shall my righteous Servant justify many;
  For He shall bear their iniquities."
"He hath poured out His soul unto death:
  And He was numbered with the transgressors;
  And He bore the sin of many,
  And made intercession for the transgressors."

As we study these statements in the light of the Gospel narratives of the crucifixion, we see how fully the plan of God was carried out in every detail, and ample provision was made for the redemption of this lost world.

In reading a book by Mr. John Stevenson, written nearly a century ago, I found some suggestions for meditation on the scenes of Calvary which may be helpful:

"Endeavor to bring fully before your mind—

"1. The sufferer,—the Lord Jesus Christ, God over all, in your nature, dying as your surety.

"2. The cause of the suffering, sin,—your sin, and the sin of the world.

"3. The agents,—the law, Satan, man, and God.

"4. The reality of Christ's sufferings,—not a mere appearance of sorrow, but a real, acute, and exquisite sense of bodily agony and of mental anguish.

"5. The place,—Golgotha, the hill of skulls; Calvary, the mount without the walls of Jerusalem, where criminals were put to death.

"6. The circumstances,—a public execution, three crosses, and three crucified thereon, two for theft, One in the midst, for sedition and blasphemy, even Jesus our blessed Saviour, condemned alike in the spiritual and criminal courts of His native country: His back, excoriated by the scourge, pressing on the wood, His hands and feet pierced with nails, His sufferings mocked, His character vilified, His strength exhausted, His soul deserted, and His spirit assailed by the temptations of Satan."

The other special chapter alluded to in the Old Testament which reveals the sufferings of Christ is the twenty-second psalm. Here we have the Saviour's own description, through His inspired prophet, of the experiences through which He would pass while on the cross.

Let us first briefly notice, with but little comment, the events of the cross, that we may have a more concrete setting for a study of that mighty victory which will be the science and the song of the universe throughout all eternity.

"They bring Him unto the place Golgotha, which is, being interpreted, The place of a skull. And they gave Him to drink wine mingled with myrrh: but He received it not. And when they had crucified Him, they parted His garments, casting lots upon them, what every man should take. And it was the third hour, and they crucified Him." Mark 15:22-25.

Thus we understand that Jesus was brought to the place of crucifixion about nine o'clock in the morning. While He was being nailed to the cross, He prayed for His murderers.

59

"Then said Jesus, Father, forgive them; for they know not what they do." Luke 23:34.

It was probably near midday when Jesus accepted the prayer of the penitent thief.

"He said unto Jesus, Lord, remember me when Thou comest into Thy kingdom. And Jesus said unto him, Verily I say unto thee, Today shalt thou be with Me in Paradise." Luke 23:42, 43.

Shortly after this He gave His mother into the care of the disciple John.

"When Jesus therefore saw His mother, and the disciple standing by, whom He loved, He saith unto His mother, Woman, behold thy son! Then saith He to the disciple, Behold thy mother! And from that hour that disciple took her unto his own home." John 19:26, 27.

About noon the supernatural darkness began.

"When the sixth hour was come, there was darkness over the whole land until the ninth hour." Mark 15:33.

For about three hours no voice broke the silence, and no ray of light pierced the darkness that covered the land. Then about three o'clock the Saviour cried out with a loud voice.

"Now from the sixth hour there was darkness over all the land unto the ninth hour. And about the ninth hour Jesus cried with a loud voice, saying, Eli, Eli, lama sabachthani? that is to say, My God, My God, why hast Thou forsaken Me?" Matt. 27:45, 46.

Evidently in a few moments the darkness lifted, and Jesus spoke again.

"When Jesus therefore had received the vinegar, He said, It is finished." John 19:30.

Immediately afterward came the last words from the cross.

"And when Jesus had cried with a loud voice, He said, Father, into Thy hands I commend My spirit: and having said thus, He gave up the ghost." Luke 23:46.

What was passing through the mind of Jesus during those long hours of silence and darkness? It is impossible for us even to imagine. But at the close of those three hours, His grief burst forth in a loud and piercing cry. We turn to the twenty-second psalm and find revealed something of what passed through His mind the next few moments. Centuries before, that cry from the cross had been recorded by the prophet of God. "My God, My God, why hast Thou forsaken Me?"

It is said that in ancient times it was customary for some person to repeat audibly the first verse or the opening words of a psalm, and then for others to join in, repeating the remainder of the psalm audibly or mentally. The whole psalm is a prayer of such supernatural intensity and power that we can only conceive of its origin in the mind of Christ. We have reason to believe that after speaking these first words audibly, He proceeded to pray through the whole psalm during the following moments. How could this prayer have been offered appropriately at any other time in the world, or by any other person who has ever lived? If Jesus did not repeat the remainder of the psalm to God as His burning appeal and supplication, when could it ever have been offered to God as a prayer?

How much of spiritual experience might be gained by the children of God if they would take time often to study this psalm, and visualize all its solemn utterances! From the midst of that mysterious darkness that enshrouded the cross, there suddenly rang out a loud, piercing cry, uttered in tones of anguish such as had never fallen upon the ears of men or angels before, "My God, My God, why hast Thou forsaken Me?"

Let us pause in solemn awe and contemplate the meaning of these mysterious words. How amazing and dreadful is the thought they convey! To think of an intelligent, rational being forsaken of God, and yet crying out in prayer to Him! And then to think who

61

this was who uttered the prayer—the One of whom God had testified on two different occasions, "This is My beloved Son, in whom I am well pleased." Now He is apparently forsaken of God, yet praying to Him with unutterable pathos. He is the One who took your place and mine, who bore our sins out into the darkness of abandonment and despair.

For many hours He had been the object of bitterest hatred, of taunts and jeers, of smiting and spitting, and such inhuman abuse as only men inspired by demons could inflict. He had been tried by an earthly tribunal both religious and civil, had been unjustly condemned, and now men have done their worst, having nailed Him to the cross, and, lifting it up, thrust it violently into the place prepared for it.

But while His body is thus tortured with excruciating pain, and His mind harassed by the disappointment and sorrow of abandonment by human friends, He is brought in spirit before the great tribunal of heaven for trial at the bar of God. The eternal Judge came down to Calvary, and set up that court where the souls of men are tried. It was the great judgment day for the sinner's Substitute. The divine Judge had "laid upon Him the iniquity of us all," and now, looking upon that appalling burden of guilt, He must inevitably let the law take its course. He could not deliver His beloved Son, for He had "made Him to be sin for us, who knew no sin; that we might be made the righteousness of God in Him." As God pronounced the sentence and turned away His face, there burst from the lips of Jesus the bitterest cry that had ever been heard in the universe, "My God, My God, why hast Thou forsaken Me?"

During those hours of darkness Christ was assailed by Satan and all the forces of the rebel leader. But it was not His physical sufferings, nor the desertion by His friends, nor the assaults of Satan, nor even the sins of the world, which wrung from His lips that exceeding bitter cry. There was something infinitely worse than all these, against which He had wrestled during those dark hours in Gethsemane, repeating over and over the cry, "My Father, if it be possible, let this cup pass from Me." He had been unmoved by all the unfeeling mockery of the crowd; He had given the loving assurance to the penitent thief. Now through those long hours of darkness and silence He had been drinking the cup against which He had prayed in the garden.

Jesus had left His position of power and glory at the right hand of God, and had come to earth as a little babe, thus identifying Himself with sinful humanity, that He might be their Saviour. Step by step through the years of childhood, youth, and young manhood, He had qualified Himself to be a merciful and faithful high priest who could be "touched with the feeling of our infirmities." He had spent years in patient and sympathetic ministry to the poor, the sick, and the despairing. All this He had done voluntarily, and now He had come to that hour when, as the sinner's substitute, He must descend into the outer darkness of God-abandonment. In response to His cry of sorrow and despair, no answer came from God the Father.

I have often tried to sense how that cry of anguish must have rent the heart of Mary, the mother of Jesus. In His infancy the messenger of the Lord had said to her, "Yea, a sword shall pierce through thy own soul also," but she little knew at that time what the experience would be. And how that cry must have wrung the hearts of Christ's disciples who were scattered among the crowd! With what sickening pain must the beloved disciple have looked upon his dying Master, and heard that piteous plea! But above all others, how must that cry have pierced the heart of the Father!

Only recently a young lady said to me, "I wish you could tell me how I can learn to love God the Father. I can love Jesus; I can understand Him; He died for me, and His life and ministry and companionship seem real; but the Father seems so remote and unreal. I do not know how to love Him."

Surely the contemplation of the scenes of Calvary should awaken love in the sinner's heart for the Father. It seems to me that any true human father could understand how much easier it would be to lay down his own life for another, than to surrender up his beloved child to die a dreadful death in behalf of a criminal. What infinite love must have constrained the heart of God as He yielded up His Son to die for a race of sinners! How can we contemplate such a sacrifice and not love Him in return?

But that cry from the cross must have struck terror and consternation to the heart of Satan and all the hosts of evil. Though they had concentrated against Him all the malignant powers of darkness, yet in the hour of supreme crisis He still prayed, His spirit cried to God, His faith held.

There are three questions in this final prayer of Christ:

"Why hast Thou forsaken Me?"
"Why art Thou so far from helping Me,
"And from the words of My roaring?"   Ps. 22:1.

We may not be able to understand nor answer these questions fully, but we may know enough to sense their deep significance, and to increase our interest in the study of what is revealed. Why *had* God forsaken Him? Since God had laid upon Him the iniquities of us all, it was necessary that He should recognize Christ as the sin bearer. The only way He could do this was to turn away from His Son, and visit the wages of sin upon Him. That expresses God's recognition of sin, His attitude toward sin. In thus turning from His own beloved Son, God showed how revolting sin is to Him. In what way could He so deeply impress the onlooking universe with the deadly, malignant nature of sin? He could not tolerate it even in His only-begotten Son. He also thus demonstrated the immutability of the divine law. That law, which is holy, just, and good, demands the death of the sinner; and when Jesus took upon Him the sins of men, the Father must turn away from Him.

"Why art Thou so far from helping Me?" What divine self-restraint it must have required on the part of the Father to withhold aid from His Son in the awful extremity of His suffering! But in the eternal ages the justice and righteousness of all God's ways will be fully vindicated.

There was a time when discord existed in heaven. Lucifer, one of the most exalted of the angels, became jealous of the position occupied by the Son of God, and determined that he would be exalted above Christ. There was war in heaven, and Lucifer and his sympathizers were cast out; but the issue was not finally settled at that time. The fallen Lucifer introduced his rebellion into this world, and for ages had carried on his insidious schemes to thwart the plans of God to rescue humanity. From the hour of Christ's birth on earth, this mighty rebel chief had marshaled all his forces against the Saviour, seeking to discourage Him and overthrow His work, and if possible destroy His life. At the time of the crucifixion the controversy had reached its supreme crisis, and the question of supremacy was to be eternally settled. Through endless ages the redeemed of earth will ascribe glory and honor and praise to Him who triumphed over sin for us.

"Why art Thou so far . . . from the words of My roaring?" In the fifth chapter of Hebrews we read: "Though He were a Son, yet learned He obedience by the things which He suffered." It was necessary that He should suffer that He might learn obedience, or experience obedience for all our disobedience. Through this suffering He was being qualified to be the Captain of our salvation. It was because "He humbled Himself, and became obedient unto death, even the death of the cross," that "God also hath highly exalted Him, and given Him a name which is above every name: that at the name of Jesus every knee should bow, of things in heaven, and things in earth, and things under the earth; and that every tongue should confess that Jesus Christ is Lord, to the glory of God the Father."

Returning to the twenty-second psalm, we continue our study of His prayer: "O My God, I cry in the daytime, but Thou hearest not; and in the night season, and am not silent." Many a night Jesus had spent in prayer, and His gracious ministry of healing and restoration day by day witnessed to the prevailing power of His prayers. But the sorrowful prayer extending over those dark hours in Gethsemane, of which this is a continuation, seemed unanswered still. Notwithstanding all the mystery of darkness and silence, there came from His heart the note of unwavering confidence in the righteousness and justice of His Father. "But Thou art holy, O Thou that inhabitest the praises of Israel."

Immediately He urged an unanswerable argument, touching in its childlike simplicity and appeal: "Our fathers trusted in Thee: they trusted, and Thou didst deliver them. They cried unto Thee, and were delivered: they trusted in Thee, and were not confounded."

And now He looks at Himself in His pitiable condition, and seeks to justify the Father: "But I am a worm, and no man; a reproach of men, and despised of the people." As He looked at His poor, pain-racked body, He recognized the helplessness of humanity. How utterly powerless is the flesh to aid the spirit! Man may glory in his physical strength, but the day inevitably comes when he recognizes it is but animate dust of the earth—just a worm.

Have we any true conception of the unspeakable condescension of Jesus Christ, the Son of God, in coming down and linking Himself with humanity? Can you imagine yourself, your nature, your mind, with the functions of a rational and cultured intellect and emotions and will, confined in a worm of the dust? What inexpressible degradation it would be to put your intelligent human personality into a worm! Yet how utterly inadequate is such a suggestion to represent the condescension of the Son of the infinite God to come and dwell in this poor human flesh! How appropriately may we, in the presence of that cross, prostrate ourselves before our Redeemer, and say, "I am a worm, and no man."

In verses 7 to 18 the Saviour describes the scenes that would be enacted by the unfeeling throng about the cross,—the cruel mockery and taunts and jeers, and the awful extremity of helplessness and suffering to which He had come. But this only increases the intensity and perseverance of His prayer, which reaches its climax in verses 19-25:

"But be not Thou far from Me, O Lord: O My strength, haste Thee to help Me. Deliver My soul from the sword; My darling from the power of the dog. Save Me from the lion's mouth: for Thou hast heard Me from the horns of the unicorn." The twenty-first verse is also rendered, "Save Me from the lion's mouth, from the horns of the unicorns. *Thou hast heard Me.*"

It is evident that this marks the turning point in this great struggle upon the cross. It marks the farthest limit of the Saviour's suffering, when the tide turned, and by a mighty effort He reached up the hand of faith through the darkness, and laid hold of God and claimed the eternal victory. At that moment when the whole universe seemed to be against Him; when all was darkness about Him; when no angel came to sustain Him; when the devil was battling against Him with all his forces; when even the face of God was turned away, He looked up with the eyes of faith and said, "God hath heard Me." From this point to the close of the prayer there is a clear note of victory. By faith He looked forward to the day when He would stand with those whom He had redeemed and adopted, in the presence of God. "I will declare Thy name unto My brethren: in the midst of the congregation will I praise Thee."

Then He concluded this triumphant prayer with the words, "They shall come, and shall declare His righteousness unto a people that shall be born, that He hath done this."

The last word of this verse is supplied, so that it should read, "He hath done," which is also rendered, "It is finished."

Thus the first verse begins with the loud cry of agony, "My God, My God, why hast Thou forsaken Me?" and the last ends with the second loud cry, "It is finished." "Father, into Thy hands I commend My spirit."

May we not see in this chapter something of what occurred in the experience of Jesus during those moments of supreme crisis in His sacrifice for us? It begins in the darkest moment, when the hiding of His Father's face seemed unendurable; and closes with the expression of unwavering confidence in the Father's acceptance of His sacrifice, and of everlasting victory and joy for His church.

"Amid the awful darkness, apparently forsaken of God, Christ had drained the last dregs in the cup of human woe. In those dreadful hours He had relied upon the evidence of His Father's acceptance heretofore given Him. He was acquainted with the character of His Father, He understood His justice, His mercy, and His great love. By faith He rested in Him whom it had ever been His joy to obey. And as in submission He committed Himself to God, the sense of the loss of His Father's favor was withdrawn. By faith, Christ was victor."—*"The Desire of Ages," p. 756.*

In the midst of the awful darkness His faith was completely triumphant, and God testified at last to the victory that was His. O for the faith of Jesus! Years later the apostle Paul wrote, "I am crucified with Christ; nevertheless I live; yet not I, but Christ liveth in me: and the life which I now live in the flesh I live by the faith of the Son of God, who loved me, and gave Himself for me." This is the faith we need, and the faith He is ever ready to impart. It is "the faith of Jesus" inseparably coupled with the "commandments of God" in the remnant church. It is expressed in the poem:

"O for a faith that will not shrink,
    Though pressed by many a foe;
That will not tremble on the brink
    Of poverty or woe;

"That will not murmur or complain
    Beneath the chastening rod,
But in the hour of grief or pain
    Can lean upon its God.

"A faith that shines more bright and clear
    When tempests rage without;
That when in danger knows no fear,
    In darkness feels no doubt;

"That bears unmoved the world's dread frown,
    Nor heeds its scornful smile;
That sin's wild ocean cannot drown,
    Nor its soft arts beguile.

"Lord, give me such a faith as this,
    And then, whate'er may come,
I'll taste e'en here the hallowed bliss
    Of an eternal home."

The Crucifixion

BEHOLD upon the shameful cross
  The spotless Victim dies.
'Mid cruel foes He yields His breath,
  A precious, priceless sacrifice.

The pitying sun withdraws his face,
  And shades of darkest night
Their black and dismal mantles throw
  Upon Mount Calvary's rugged height.

The flinty rocks are rent in twain!
  The graves give up their trust;
And sleeping saints immortal rise
  Victorious from the silent dust.

Inanimate creation groans,
  And pitying angels weep,
And o'er the Master's lonely tomb
  Their solemn, sacred vigil keep.

O pitying Christ! O Lamb of God!
  And didst Thou die for me?
Then let my hand forget her skill
  If I forget thee, CALVARY.

      —*Mrs. L. D. A. Stuttle.*

THE CROSS AND THE CRUCIFIXION

"SUSPENDED on the cross!   On His pale brow
Hang the cold drops of death; through ev'ry limb
The piercing torture rages; ev'ry nerve,
Stretched with excess of pain, trembles convulsed.
Now look beneath, and view the senseless crowd;
How they deride His sufferings, how they shake
Their heads contemptuous, while the bitter taunt,
More bitter than the gall they gave, insults
The agony of Him on whom they gaze.
But hark!   He speaks, and the still hovering breath
Wafts His last prayer to all-approving heaven;
'Forgive them, for they know not what they do.' "

In gaining a true understanding of the atoning sacrifice of Christ, it is necessary to study carefully the distinction between the cross and the crucifixion. The scripture states that Christ, "through the eternal Spirit offered Himself without spot to God," to take the sinner's place and suffer the penalty of the violated law. This was also the Father's plan, and so Christ came in harmony with "the determinate counsel and fore-knowledge of God."

While it was the purpose of the Father that Jesus should make a voluntary offering of His life to redeem the fallen race, it was never His plan that the very ones for whom He was making this infinite sacrifice, should put their Saviour to a violent and shameful death. It was not God's choice that Judas should betray His Lord, nor that the religious leaders of the chosen nation should deny Him "in the presence of Pilate, when he was determined to let Him go," and desire "a murderer to be granted unto them." Nevertheless, having committed Himself to the task of reconciling the world to God, the Saviour was willing to endure whatever Satan and sin might interpose to thwart the divine plan.

Many have such a superficial view of the atonement that they regard the physical death of Jesus as a direct result of the crucifixion, and regard that death as the sacrifice which atones for our sins. There is a wide distinction between the voluntary sacrificial offering of Christ by which we are redeemed, and the diabolical crime of men in publicly executing Him on the cross.

Christ taken by wicked hands and slain, is the greatest of all crimes the universe has known. It was the climax of sin and rebellion, and was no necessary part of God's plan for man's salvation. Christ's voluntary offering of His life for sinners, is the most sublime moral act of all eternity.

The cross, as it represents the voluntary sacrifice of Christ, reveals the infinite measure of the love of God, and the inconceivable length to which He was willing to go for our redemption. The crucifixion represents the fiendish, malignant nature of sin, from which the atoning sacrifice of Christ alone can save us.

It makes a very great difference whether we think of the crucifixion as a diabolical work of men, which was necessary for our salvation, or as a tragedy brought about by the opposition of human and satanic agencies against a voluntary work of God to save sinners. God's plan embraced the sacrifice of His Son as our substitute and sin bearer, but it is unthinkable that He should devise a plan that would make it necessary for Judas to betray Him or for cruel men to put Him to death. Nevertheless, God knew that the hatred and opposition of men and demons would result in the denial and crucifixion of Christ, and He permitted it, and in His infinite wisdom and power He has ordained that it shall be one of the most potent factors in arousing the moral sensibilities of men and bringing conviction and repentance.

Many seem to think little about the cross beyond its physical aspects. It brings to them a picture of Christ with arms outstretched and with wounds and blood on head, hands, feet, and side. The vision which is restricted to mere mortal agony entirely misses the significance of the vicarious offering. It is essential that we look beyond the human tragedy, and apprehend the spiritual and mediatorial transaction between the Father and the Son. The unspeakable cruelty of men and the agony and shame of the innocent victim awaken our sympathy, but it is the realization of the atoning work of Christ that brings an awful sense of guilt, and leads to repentance and self-humiliation.

The cross and the curse and death belong to the sinner. Left to himself, he must carry the burden of guilt into the outer darkness of God-abandonment and despair, where "there is weeping and gnashing of teeth." But when Jesus went to the cross, He attained that identity with sinners which enabled the Father to lay our sins upon Him, and His righteousness upon us. Thus the cross is the actual and only meeting place between God and man. In the mysterious union formed between the sinner and Christ at the cross, the Saviour bears away the guilt, and the sinner receives the righteousness of Christ. O wondrous provision of divine grace!

"Without the cross, man could have no union with the Father. On it depends our every hope. From it shines the light of the Saviour's love; and when at the foot of the cross the sinner looks up to the One who died to save him, he may rejoice with fullness of joy; for his sins are pardoned. Kneeling in faith at the cross, he has reached the highest place to which man can attain."—*"The Acts of the Apostles," pp. 209, 210.*

There were many classes represented in the great throng that surrounded the cross. The gospel narrative records representative statements from these various classes, all of which reveal the erroneous views held and their utter blindness regarding the character of the events taking place before their eyes.

"They that passed by railed on Him, wagging their heads, and saying, Ah, Thou that destroyest the temple, and buildest it in three days, save Thyself, and come down from the cross."

Probably a large majority in that great multitude entertained the common error that no one will suffer if he can possibly avoid it. The very fact that Christ remained on the cross was sufficient evidence to these superficial people that He was powerless to help Himself. To them He was a deluded fanatic, or an impostor, who had been caught in the meshes of fate and was suffering the consequences of His folly.

"Likewise also the chief priests mocking said among themselves with the scribes, He saved others; Himself He cannot save. Let Christ the King of Israel descend now from the cross, that we may see and believe."

What amazing spiritual blindness of the religious leaders of the nation! It was at their demand that the crime was being committed. Their ignorance of the first principles of salvation was revealed in their mockery of the dying Saviour. They admitted that He saved others, but could not see that this made it impossible to save Himself. Had He accepted their challenge and saved Himself, all mankind would be forever lost. They were the priests and leaders who were familiar with centuries of typical sacrifices of unnumbered lambs as a representation of the substitutionary sacrifice of the promised Messiah, the Lamb of God. And now that the real sacrifice for sin was being made, they were mocking and jeering at Him.

"One of the malefactors which were hanged railed on Him, saying, If Thou be Christ, save Thyself and us."

It seems little wonder that when the religious leaders and representatives of the people failed utterly to discern the true significance of the sacrifice, this poor criminal should see only the human tragedy. But it is also a solemn warning to men against blindly follow-

74

ing a religious hierarchy without a personal knowledge and understanding of the light of God.

"The soldiers also mocked Him, coming to Him, and offering Him vinegar, and saying, If Thou be the King of the Jews, save Thyself."

In that dread hour the universe looked on in solemn silence and dismay, and a pall of darkness fell over the earth in token of the sympathy of inanimate nature with its suffering and expiring Author. Man alone, with a heart unfeeling as adamant, mocked and scoffed and derided the Christ.

From the great throng the cry, "Save Thyself," arose to His ears again and again, testifying to the blindness of all those human witnesses who saw only a dying man, and supposed this to be the end.

But there was a single exception to this almost universal blindness. Among all the mocking voices crying, "Save Thyself," one solitary man cried, "Save me."

"One of the malefactors which were hanged railed on Him, saying, If Thou be Christ, save Thyself and us. But the other answering rebuked him, saying, Dost not thou fear God, seeing thou art in the same condemnation? And we indeed justly; for we receive the due reward of our deeds: but this man hath done nothing amiss. And he said unto Jesus, Lord, remember me when Thou comest into Thy kingdom."

The poor dying thief called Him Lord. He alone among all that vast throng recognized Jesus as the Saviour. He saw something transpiring that others did not see. For centuries God's chosen people had brought the innocent lamb to the temple daily. Men laid their hands upon its head, and confessed their sins, and it was slain as a type of the atoning sacrifice of that One who was to come. Now He is here, and the great antitypical offering is being made. He is "wounded for our transgressions," He is "bruised for our iniquities," "and the Lord hath laid on Him the iniquity of us all."

But only the dying thief understood. He saw in

Jesus the Good Shepherd laying down His life for the sheep, and he realized that if Christ should save Himself, the human race would be lost. He also saw a kingdom beyond the darkness and agony and death of Jesus, into which he might enter at last by virtue of that death.

Probably the mother of Jesus, and all His friends and disciples who might be looking on, hoped that He would descend from the cross. Because of a lack of discernment of what God was doing, they would doubtless have taken Him down had it been possible, and have prevented Him from finishing the work He had undertaken to perform.

But the poor thief understood. He saw the fulfillment of that promise toward which the sacrifice of an unblemished lamb by a sinner had pointed forward for four thousand years. He saw in Jesus the Lamb of God that taketh away the sins of the world. He saw beyond the dreadful crime against the Innocent One the great reality that Christ was bearing our sins in His own body on the tree. He saw the human pain and agony, in which he also shared; but beyond that he saw what others did not see,—a great transaction between the Father and His Son, by which the sins of men were dealt with and disposed of to the satisfaction of the Father, and a way of escape made for sinners. He saw the Saviour reconciling man to God, and opening the way into His eternal kingdom. For a place in that kingdom he made request. "And he said unto Jesus, Lord, remember me when Thou comest into Thy kingdom."

Instantly came the ringing assurance, "Verily I say unto thee, Today shalt thou be with Me in Paradise."

Thus God ever rewards true faith. One who could look at the Man on the cross, dying an ignominious death in company with vile criminals, and believe in Him, and pray to Him as the promised Saviour and King, possessed a faith which God honors.

Evidently the physical death of Jesus was not the

result of the crucifixion, but was a voluntary laying down of His life in harmony with the divine plan. Death by means of crucifixion was a long, lingering process, requiring many hours, and usually some days. Joseph of Arimathæa "went to Pilate, and begged the body of Jesus." "Pilate marveled if He were already dead."

Jesus had declared to His disciples that His death depended upon Himself. "I am the good shepherd: the good shepherd giveth His life for the sheep." "As the Father knoweth Me, even so know I the Father: and I lay down My life for the sheep." "Therefore doth My Father love Me, because I lay down My life, that I might take it again. No man taketh it from Me, but I lay it down of Myself. I have power to lay it down, and I have power to take it again. This commandment have I received of My Father." John 10:11, 15, 17, 18.

Jesus said, "Father, into Thy hands I commend My spirit: and having said thus, He gave up the ghost." When He had fully carried out the terms of the agreement with the Father for the salvation of men, He surrendered up His physical life. It is true that men were just as guilty before God of the murder of Jesus as though their hands had taken His life, for the guilt lies in the intention and will. In their wills and hearts they killed Him. Nevertheless, His life was not taken from Him, but was voluntarily laid down as a propitiation for our sins.

The historic crucifixion represents the attitude of men toward Christ. The cross—the voluntary sacrifice of His life—represents the attitude of God toward men. That crucifixion was local in time and place, yet it was world wide in application, and it embodied a great principle.

"The whole world stands charged today with the deliberate rejection and murder of the Son of God. The Word bears record that Jews and Gentiles, kings, governors, ministers, priests, and people,—all classes and sects who reveal the same spirit of envy, hatred, prejudice, and unbelief manifested by those who put to death the Son of God,—would act the same part were the opportunity granted, as did the Jews and people of the time of Christ. They would be partakers of the same spirit that demanded the death of the Son of God."

"The world is soon to be judged. A righteous God must avenge the death of His Son. Today men are choosing Barabbas, and saying, Crucify Christ. . . . Those who today despise the law of Jehovah, showing no respect for His commandments, are taking sides with the great apostate. They proclaim to a sin-corrupted world that the law of God is null and void. Those who declare this as truth deceive the people, and have virtually nailed the law of Jehovah to the cross between two thieves. . . . Before the worlds unfallen, and the heavenly universe, the world will have to give an account to the Judge of the whole earth, the very one they condemned and crucified. What a reckoning day that will be! It is the great day of God's vengeance. Christ does not then stand at Pilate's bar. Pilate and Herod, and all that mocked, scourged, rejected, and crucified Him, will then understand what it means to feel the wrath of the Lamb."—*"Testimonies to Ministers," pp. 131, 132.*

As we kneel in faith at the cross day by day, let us seek to see beyond the humiliation and shame, beyond the physical torture and suffering, of Jesus. Let us pray for divine illumination, that we may comprehend more and more that spiritual and mediatorial work by which we are reconciled to God through the death of His Son. Let us learn by experience what it means that "He made Him to be sin for us, who knew no sin, that we might be made the righteousness of God in Him."

THE CROSS AND SIN

The terrible havoc sin has wrought in us can be realized only in the presence of the awful tragedy of Calvary. The dreadful and inevitable consequences of sin may be judged by the unspeakable cost of redemption. Our appreciation of the atonement will be in proportion to our realization of the horror of that evil which made the atonement necessary. We need to be awakened to sense the deadly, malignant nature of the sin from which there was no escape but by way of Gethsemane and Calvary.

Those who are familiar with the Scriptures will recognize the definition of sin given by the apostle John: "Whosoever committeth sin transgresseth the law: for sin is the transgression of the law." Sin as an act, is the transgression of the law. But we are living in an age of lawlessness. Many laws of the land are of secondary importance, and are transgressed daily through ignorance or carelessness. Hundreds of men who commit the most serious infractions of the law escape with little or no punishment.

The tendency of these things is to minimize in our minds the seriousness of the matter of lawbreaking. We readily forget that it is not possible to transgress the slightest detail of the divine law without entailing the most terrible consequences. The transgressor of civil law is a criminal. The transgressor of the divine law is a moral criminal. He is lawless. Hence it is the moral law of ten commandments which points out sin, and without the law there would be no consciousness of sin, and no transgression.

The moral law is an expression of the character of God. It is a law of love, mercy, truth, and holiness. Therefore the sinner is antagonistic, not only to the government of God as expressed in the letter of the law, but also to His character—His love, purity, truth, and goodness.

There is only one remedy for sin as a violation of the law of Jehovah. "All we like sheep have gone astray; we have turned every one to his own way; and the Lord hath laid on Him the iniquity of us all." "Who His own self bare our sins in His own body on the tree." Jesus is the great sin bearer, and those who accept Him are absolved from their burden of sins. Our acts of transgression constitute us moral criminals against the government of God, and bring upon us the condemnation of death. We can escape this only by accepting Christ as our substitute and sin bearer, for He died in our place. As we thus by faith bring our sins to the cross, we believe that God for Christ's sake freely pardons them all. But pardon does not change us. It simply changes our relation to the law.

There is a great difference between sins and sin. Many find serious difficulty in their Christian life because they do not understand this distinction. Beneath all our acts of transgression is the principle of sin from which they spring. Though all our evil deeds were pardoned, we would still go on sinning. Something more must be done for us than simply to pardon our sins.

A man is thrown into prison for murder. Through the clemency of the governor he is pardoned and released. But no sooner is he free than he commits another murder. This is repeated again and again. Intelligent people would say that such a course is utterly unreasonable. It would not be just or right to pardon a man unless some change could be wrought in him which would take from him the disposition to take another life.

Thus it is in God's dealing with sinful men. He is

willing to pardon the transgressor, but this would avail nothing unless a change is wrought in the man's nature. He must remove from the man that which caused him to sin. This brings us to another aspect of sin as set forth in the Scriptures.

"Wash you, make you clean; put away the evil of your doings from before Mine eyes; cease to do evil; learn to do well; seek judgment, relieve the oppressed, judge the fatherless, plead for the widow. Come now, and let us reason together, saith the Lord: though your sins be as scarlet, they shall be as white as snow; though they be red like crimson, they shall be as wool." Isa. 1:16-18.

The pardon of our sins changes our relation to the law. It removes the condemnation, but it does not change our nature. We are powerless to refrain from repeating the offense. There is an additional work that must be done. Our hearts are unclean. The very fountain of our nature is impure and unholy. Sin has wrought more in us than merely making us guilty in the sight of the law. It has wrought moral degeneracy. It has introduced a moral poison into our human nature. And so the inspired prophet cries, "O Jerusalem, wash thine heart from wickedness, that thou mayest be saved. How long shall thy vain thoughts lodge within thee?"

What a conflict we passed through when there came to us a revelation of the purity and holiness of God, and the noble and exalted character of our Saviour, and with it an awful conviction of our own condition! What a struggle with that constant stream of thought, —frivolous, selfish, impure,—ever welling up as from a fountain, bringing perpetual shame and condemnation! What hours there have been, when in the presence of divine purity we have hated and despised ourselves, and wept in anguish because of our helplessness against that deadly stream of thought!

Thank God, He has made provision for every form and aspect of sin. "Though we walk in the flesh, we

6   81

do not war after the flesh: (for the weapons of our war-fare are not carnal, but mighty through God to the pulling down of strongholds;) casting down imaginations, and every high thing that exalteth itself against the knowledge of God, and bringing into captivity every thought to the obedience of Christ."

The Saviour said, "From within, out of the heart of men, proceed evil thoughts, adulteries, fornications, murders, thefts, covetousness, wickedness, deceit, lasciviousness, an evil eye, blasphemy, pride, foolishness."

These all come from the heart, but the promise of deliverance and victory covers them all. The heart can be cleansed, the fountain purified. The saints of old recognized the necessity for this cleansing, and for it they fervently prayed: "Wash me thoroughly from mine iniquity, and cleanse me from my sin." "Purge me with hyssop, and I shall be clean: wash me, and I shall be whiter than snow." "Create in me a clean heart, O God; and renew a right spirit within me."

Well may we men pray for purity of heart. We all have mothers, or sisters, or wives, or daughters, whom we love. We like to think that their hearts and minds are pure and clean and white. But why should we except or desire their hearts to be purer than our own? Why should not we men have our hearts cleansed and made as pure and clean as we think theirs should be? God says, "Though your sins be as scarlet, they shall be as white as snow." He means us to understand that nothing, not even the heart of an angel, could be whiter than He will make our hearts if we will let Him. This is exactly what Jesus Christ will do for the vilest sinner who truly accepts Him as He is presented in the gospel. Paul gives us an illustration of this mighty miracle:

Paul had a disappointing experience in Athens, and when he reached Corinth, there was a great passion burning in his heart to see men and women saved. Later he wrote them that he came to them with a great determination not to know anything among them save Jesus Christ and Him crucified. He had a great crowd gathered before him. Among them were men and women who were idolaters, others were thieves, some were adulterers, others were murderers, and others were guilty of the foulest and most degrading vices. But as He preached Christ crucified, a mighty power took hold of those poor heathen people. They repented of their sins, and were pardoned; but God did not stop there, as Paul so earnestly testified in writing them later:

"Know ye not that the unrighteous shall not inherit the kingdom of God? Be not deceived: neither fornicators, nor idolaters, nor adulterers, . . . nor thieves, nor covetous, nor drunkards, nor revilers, nor extortioners, shall inherit the kingdom of God. *And such were some of you: but ye are washed, but ye are sanctified, but ye are justified in the name of the Lord Jesus, and by the Spirit of our God."*

The apostle John mentions this twofold work of dealing with our sins. "If we confess our sins, He is faithful and just to *forgive us our sins,* and to *cleanse us from all unrighteousness."*

Christ's death on the cross, bearing our iniquities, our acts of transgression, enables Him to take all the guilt and condemnation from us when we come to Him in faith. Then we must come for the further work by which His blood washes our poor sin-polluted hearts, taking from us all that is impure and unholy, all the pride, selfishness, foolishness, love of the world, and desire to sin, leaving them pure and clean and fit for His indwelling.

Even after our sins are all forgiven and our hearts cleansed at the springs of thought and character, there is much God needs to do for us. As we study His word and seek to do His will, we shall be conscious of spiritual infirmity and disability which we shall long to have removed, and we shall pray as did David, "Lord, be merciful unto me: *heal my soul;* for I have sinned against Thee." Sin produces disease and deformity of the spiritual being. The Saviour said, "They that are whole have no need of the physician, but they that are sick: I came not to call the righteous, but sinners to repentance." He recognized that men and women in slavery to sin were suffering the ravages of a fearful disease, a malady of the soul which assumes myriad forms. He looked upon sinners with sorrow and compassion, and longed to heal their souls.

There are many forms of physical disease, and there seem to be corresponding spiritual maladies. With what pity do we look upon the physically blind! It is comforting to know that the Saviour looks upon the spiritually blind with equal compassion and sympathy. There are human beings who are physically deaf, others who are dumb, others are afflicted with leprosy, cancer, tumor, and a hundred acute and chronic diseases. Only a brief consideration will bring to mind the counterpart of each disease and deformity in the spiritual being.

How appropriate that I should pray "Lord, be merciful unto me: heal my soul; for I have sinned against Thee"! That sin which I took into my soul has had the effect of paralyzing it, of blinding it, of deafening it, of maiming it, so that it is deformed and defective and sick.

One can easily discover that Christ's miracles of healing and restoring the diseased bodies of men and women were performed primarily with the purpose of inspiring faith within them to seek healing of soul from the great Physician. Jesus yearned over the people who were sick with so many forms of the sin disease, and He wanted them to realize that He could heal them all.

A man was sick with the palsy and was brought to Jesus on a bed. "Jesus seeing their faith said unto the sick of the palsy, Son, be of good cheer; thy sins be forgiven thee." The statement was startling and unexpected. He had healed many of physical ailments, but He said to this man, "I heal your soul's diseases." The Pharisees, looking on, said among themselves, "This man blasphemeth;" for while they could not deny that He healed men physically, they refused to believe that He could heal their souls. But Jesus taught that the very miracles of physical healing were evidence of His divine power, when He said, "That ye may know that the Son of man hath power on earth to forgive sins, (then saith He to the sick of the palsy,) Arise, take up thy bed, and go unto thine house." Doubtless there were men and women looking on in whose hearts was awakened new faith in the power of Jesus to heal their soul's diseases.

"This people's heart is waxed gross, and their ears are dull of hearing, and their eyes they have closed; lest at any time they should see with their eyes, and hear with their ears, and should understand with their heart, and should be converted, and I should heal them."

Heart disease, blindness, deafness—how almost universally prevalent they are, even among those who profess to be children of God! We are reminded of the mournful cry of the prophet: "Is there no balm in Gilead; is there no physician there? why then is not the health of the daughter of my people recovered?"

Jesus is our great physician. His "hand is not shortened, that it cannot save; neither His ear heavy, that it cannot hear;" but He says that our iniquities have separated between us and Him, and we have refused to come to Him and be healed. Unless we ourselves are whole, how can we minister the healing of Christ to those who are sick?

The apostle Paul admonishes us, "Lift up the hands which hang down, and the feeble knees; and make straight paths for your feet, lest that which is lame be turned out of the way; but let it rather be healed." How many there are all about us whose hands hang down, and whose knees are feeble, who are weak and wavering and unstable, and we do not know when they are going to slip and go down and be lost forever. It is our exalted privilege to become channels for the healing power of Christ. There is a very solemn responsibility resting upon every Christian to make straight paths for his own feet, that those who are lame and halt and sick may not be turned farther away from God through his inconsistencies, but rather may be healed.

Someone may read these lines who has sincerely repented of his sins, and, having confessed them and turned them over to Christ, believes they are all pardoned. That is a glorious start, and I bid him rejoice in Christ as His sin bearer. But he may yet be distressed and perplexed by the consciousness that there is much evil within which brings him down again and again in humiliation and defeat. The spring has not been cleansed by the application of the blood of Christ. I bid him in the name of Jesus to take the next step now. Ask for the cleansing, and claim it by faith in His name. He will not fail you in this, even as He has not in the pardon. The cleansing is as truly yours through the atoning sacrifice of the cross as is the pardon.

But he may have claimed both the pardon and the cleansing and be rejoicing in the consciousness of a great deliverance, and yet be aware of a spiritual weakness or deformity or defect that makes his Christian life weak and ineffective and disappointing. Why not claim the spiritual healing also? Surely it belongs with the pardon and cleansing. It is yours as truly as the others, but it must be claimed and appropriated by faith.

God has made provision for complete deliverance from the guilt of sin, from the defilement of sin, from the disease and sickness of sin, and from the power and dominion of sin. Only when this full salvation is experienced can one rejoice in the liberty of Christ. "Men are weighed in the balance and found wanting when they are living in the practice of any known sin." —*"Testimonies to Ministers," p. 440.*

"Verily, verily, I say unto you, Whosoever committeth sin is the servant of sin. . . . If the Son therefore shall make you free, ye shall be free indeed." How can any man who is honestly obliged to admit that he is *not free,* bear witness to a real Saviour? The testimony of the angel of the Lord to Joseph was, "Thou shalt call His name Jesus: for He shall save His people from their sins." What right have we to testify that we are His children while still acknowledging that we are slaves to sin? Is not such a witness really against Him rather than for Him? On the other hand, what a power there is in the testimony of a man who can truly say, "I praise God that He saves and keeps me moment by moment as I go about in fellowship and communion with Him! Each day I rejoice in Him, for He delivers me from sins that a few months ago held me in abject slavery."

Many are struggling against the evil tendencies of their nature, or the hereditary law of sin in humanity. Paul said, "I find then a law, that, when I would do good, evil is present with me. For I delight in the law of God after the inward man: but I see another law in my members, warring against the law of my mind, and bringing me into captivity to the law of sin which is in my members." There is but one way of deliverance from the powerful tendencies of this hereditary law.

"Christ is the 'light, which lighteth every man that cometh into the world.' As through Christ every human being has life, so also through Him every soul receives some ray of divine light. Not only intellectual but spiritual power, a perception of right, a desire for goodness, exists in every heart. But against these principles there is struggling an antagonistic power. The result of the eating of a tree of knowledge of good and evil is manifest in every man's experience. There is in his nature a bent to evil, a force which, unaided, he cannot resist. To withstand this force, to attain that ideal which in his inmost soul he accepts as alone worthy, he can find help in but one power. That power is Christ."—*"Education," p. 29.*

On the cross, Christ bore our sins, and made provision for their forgiveness. He shed His blood, which can wash our impure hearts and make them clean from all defilement and impurity. Through His ministry in our behalf in heaven today the Holy Spirit comes to work the miracle of healing and restoration in our souls. And by that same Spirit the presence of Christ is made real in our hearts, to counteract completely the hereditary law of sin, and make us free in Him.

"Rest, weary soul!
The penalty is borne, the ransom paid,
For all thy sins full satisfaction made;
Strive not to do thyself what Christ has done,
Claim the free gift, and make the joy thine own;
No more by pangs of guilt and fear distressed,
Rest, sweetly rest."

CRUCIFIED WITH CHRIST

Then said Jesus unto His disciples, If any man will come after Me, let him deny himself, and take up his cross, and follow Me. For whosoever will save his life shall lose it: and whosoever will lose his life for My sake shall find it." Matt. 16:24, 25.

There are four exceedingly important and interesting points presented in this statement of our Lord:

1. Christ set up one supreme condition of discipleship.
2. It is a matter of life or death.
3. It is a matter of each individual's own choice.
4. It is to deny self, and take up the cross.

Let us seek to understand what it means to take up the cross. Remember these words were spoken to the disciples long before the Saviour had even hinted to them His coming crucifixion. Their ideas of the cross must have been the prevailing ideas of the people. Doubtless they had seen the Roman soldiers lead a condemned criminal from the prison. Outside the gates he was compelled to take up the cross, or at least one beam of the cross upon which he was to be crucified. The poor, condemned man would have to lift it onto his back, and perhaps, impelled by the sharp spear or sword or lash, carry it along the street to the place of execution. He was under sentence of death. People looked on and said, "He is going to die." He was carrying on his back the very symbol of death, the evidence that he was under sentence of death. He was doomed, and there was no escape.

That is what Jesus was talking about. "If any man

will come after Me, let him deny himself, and take up his cross, and follow Me." It is not easy for us to get the correct setting of this fundamental lesson, because the sacrifice of Christ upon the cross has changed our whole conception of its significance. To our minds today the cross represents the most sacred and holy and noble sentiments known to us. The precious memories and associations connected with Calvary inspire in our minds tender thoughts and sympathies. But when Jesus spoke those words, the mention of the cross awakened feelings of aversion and abhorrence. It was usually only the vilest and most hopeless and incorrigible of criminals who were subjected to this shameful death. The one, therefore, who died on the cross, was not only covered with disgrace and ignominy, but justly so. When Jesus went to the cross, it was because God "made Him to be sin for us." He went as the chiefest of all criminals, the representative, all-inclusive sinner. The crimes of the two crucified with Him were as a drop in the ocean compared with the burden of guilt He bore. And the penalty was just. As the sinner's substitute, He deserved it all. Thus He "condemned sin in the flesh." It is the same sin that I have in my flesh. It never changes, and for it the cross is the only remedy.

When Paul said, "God forbid that I should glory, save in the cross of our Lord Jesus Christ," he was not thinking of the glorified emblem of Christ's matchless love. He was thinking of the cross as an instrument of torture, and disgrace, and horror, and death to that which deserved to die, and he was glorying in that. It is that cross which the Lord says must be taken up by everyone who would follow Him. It is of that cross Paul was speaking when he said, "We preach Christ crucified, unto the Jews a stumbling block, and unto the Greeks foolishness."

Mark the words of the Saviour, "Whosoever will save his life [from the death of this cross] shall lose it: and whosoever will lose his life [through this cross] for My sake shall find it." Strange paradox indeed! The only way for a man to save his life is to go to the cross and lose it. Refusing the cross, he forfeits eternal life.

> "Each on his cross, by Thee we hang awhile,
> Watching Thy patient smile,
> Till we have learned to say, 'Tis justly done;
> Only in glory, Lord, Thy sinful servant own."

Here it is necessary to consider the distinction between sin and sins. Sins, acts of disobedience, transgressions of the divine law, God is always ready to forgive, through the merits of Christ, in response to the prayer of penitence and faith. But sin God cannot forgive.

Sin is the nature which leads us to disobey God's law. The nature with which we come into the world does not change, as we read in the Saviour's words: "That which is born of the flesh is flesh; and that which is born of the Spirit is spirit." The only way to be rid of a bad nature is by death. The only way to receive a good nature is to be born again.

"Christ died *for our sins.*" 1 Cor. 15:3.

"He died *unto sin.*" Rom. 6:10.

He died for our sins, so that He might be able to pardon them. He died to sin in our human nature, so that we, by sharing in that death, might be delivered from our sinful nature.

When we come to God and confess all our sins and ask forgiveness in the name of Jesus Christ, it is freely granted. But after they are all pardoned, we return to our sinful habits and our acts of disobedience, because we have this sinful nature. It is a fallen, unholy, degenerate nature. So after Christ deals with our sins and puts them away, something must be done with this sinful nature, so that we shall be delivered from the dominion of sin and from the will and desire to commit sin.

Paul said, "This we know—that our old self was

91

nailed to the cross with Him, in order that our sinful nature might be deprived of its power, so that we should no longer be the slaves of sin." Rom. 6:6, 7, Weymouth.

This "old self" is also called the "carnal mind," the "flesh," the "old man," but it all represents the same thing. This "old man" which each individual possesses by inheritance and cultivation, is the sin nature which is wholly and hopelessly and incorrigibly bad. Nothing can be done for it. The Lord makes only one provision for its disposition, and that is the cross and death.

The Scriptures tell us that we are to "put off concerning the former conversation the *old man,* which is corrupt according to the deceitful lusts;" and "put on the new man, which after God is created in righteousness and true holiness." Before conversion our lives are controlled by our selfish, sinful nature. When we accept Christ and are born again, we are to dethrone the old nature, and enthrone Him in the new nature which He creates in us.

But now we necessarily have two natures to deal with—the old degenerate flesh nature, and the new divine nature from above. It is necessary to nourish and cultivate the new nature by the means of grace so abundantly provided by our heavenly Father. It is equally necessary to crucify the "flesh." Crucify is defined as "putting to a violent and painful death." But naturally I do not want to be crucified. It is torture, suffering, agony, death. I do not want to suffer, I do not want to die.

But the Master says, "Whosoever *will* save his life shall lose it: and whosoever *will* lose his life for My sake shall find it." To this the apostle Paul adds, "They that are Christ's have crucified the flesh with the affections and lusts." It is a matter of the individual's choice, whether he will go voluntarily to the cross and lose his life, with all its vile, unholy practices and tendencies, and thus make way for the new divine life; or whether he will choose to retain the old sinful nature, and go down in eternal death.

Since my very nature is selfish and sinful, and is not subject to the law of God, neither indeed can be, how shall I ever bring myself to the place where I am willing to choose to deny and reject and mortify and crucify myself? There are two things which the Spirit of God is able to reveal to me, which will help greatly in making this decision.

He can show me through the word of God how impure, unholy, vile, and loathsome my selfish nature is.

He can show me the pure, holy, beautiful character of Jesus, and how I may have His nature by giving up my own to death.

Consider carefully these scriptures, which reveal the true character of the carnal nature:

"There is none righteous, no, not one: there is none that understandeth, there is none that seeketh after God. They are all gone out of the way, they are together become unprofitable; there is none that doeth good, no, not one. Their throat is an open sepulcher; with their tongues they have used deceit; the poison of asps is under their lips: whose mouth is full of cursing and bitterness: their feet are swift to shed blood: destruction and misery are in their ways: and the way of peace they have not known: there is no fear of God before their eyes." "All have sinned, and come short of the glory of God." Rom. 3:10-18, 23.

"I know that in me (that is, in my flesh,) dwelleth no good thing." Rom. 7:18.

It may be some have read this statement and felt that Paul must have expressed an extreme idea, or exaggerated the real facts. Others may credit his truthfulness, but be surprised to realize that he was such an unusually and extremely wicked man. But it is quite another thing for each one to realize that this is a divinely inspired statement of a truth concerning every son and daughter of Adam. By nature there is no good thing in us. Much that appears good to our unsanctified eyes is not good; and if there is any real good in us, it has been imparted through divine grace, and is not a part of our own nature.

This was a great discovery that the patriarch Job made when he had a revelation of God. "I have heard of Thee by the hearing of the ear: but now mine eye seeth Thee. Wherefore, I abhor myself." We have no true conception of what we are until we view ourselves in the presence of God. The spotless purity and infinite loveliness of the character of the Saviour in contrast with the baseness and corruption of our nature, cause us to abhor ourselves, and long for deliverance from the depravity and deformities of our sinful flesh.

"There shall ye remember your ways, and all your doings, wherein ye have been defiled; and ye shall loathe yourselves in your own sight for all your evils that ye have committed." Eze. 20:43.

When a person has a revelation of the impurity and vileness and degeneracy of his nature, which causes him to hate and abhor and loathe himself, there comes to him a new understanding of the meaning of the cross. It was because sinful human nature was so abhorrent in the sight of God that Jesus took it to the cross and death. Now it is possible for me to bring my own sinful, degenerate nature to Christ, and by faith place it on the cross with Him. Taking up the cross means taking the sentence of death upon myself. And so I say, "Lord, I agree with Thee that this self, this old man, this carnal mind, this flesh, this degenerate nature, is so vile, so unholy, so utterly and hopelessly polluted by sin, that it deserves to die, and must die, and I agree with Thee in pronouncing the sentence of death upon it. Whatever the pain, and sorrow, and agony of death it requires, I have made my choice, I am resolved to die; for Thou hast said that by way of the cross alone may I be delivered from this nature, which is doomed to death and which is death, and from Thee receive eternal life."

"Oh! hide this self from me, that I
No more, but Christ in me, may live.
My vile affections crucify,
Nor let one darling lust survive.
In all things nothing may I see,
Nothing desire or seek but Thee."

But should I choose to say, "It is too hard, too dreadful, I dare not, cannot go to that cruel cross and death," I hear ringing in my ears the solemn words of Christ, "Whosoever *will* save his life, shall lose it." Having had divine revelation of the true nature of self as it appears in the presence of infinite love and purity and unselfishness, if I still refuse to part with this degenerate self, I am lost. But by denying self and taking up the cross, the symbol of death, and concurring with God in the sentence of death upon self, I am saved.

Here is the foundation principle of the great plan of redemption. Through death comes life. Jesus died that we might have life. We die to our sinful nature, that He might impart His divine nature. *Spiritual life comes to us only through carnal death.*

Sometimes people say, "I do not see how this can apply to me. I am not very bad. I have never done anything particularly wicked." But it is not so much what we do, as what we are, that will keep us out of the kingdom of heaven. It is an easy matter for God to dispose of our sins. He can pardon them in a moment, when we confess and forsake them. But God can do nothing with our sinful nature or personality, only as we choose to let Him. There must be a voluntary acceptance of the cross, a voluntary denial of self, a crucifixion of the flesh.

Is it not plain why Christ made this the supreme condition of discipleship? It would not be possible to live for Him here, nor with Him hereafter, while our vile, degenerate, impure nature controlled our lives.

There is another precious truth which we may consider in this connection. It is the fact that as we bring our sinful nature to the cross day by day, and by faith agree to its death with Christ, He imparts His own life to us.

"Always bearing about in the body the dying of the Lord Jesus, that the life also of Jesus might be made manifest in our body." 2 Cor. 4:10.

It is the dying of our carnal nature that makes room for the impartation of the divine nature. "God forbid that I should glory, save in the cross of our Lord Jesus Christ." How could one glory in that instrument which was the symbol of shame and torture and death? Because it is the only means by which he can be delivered from his vile, loathsome, sinful nature, and in exchange receive the glorious righteousness of Christ.

The only means God has provided for the disposal of the carnal nature is the cross. On it self is to be crucified. Kneeling in faith at the cross, the sinner receives a new nature from above, and is delivered from the old nature, which is corrupt according to the deceitful lusts. The cross becomes the means of his continual freedom and victory. This is what it means to take up the cross and to be "crucified with Christ." We glory in the cross, since by it we are crucified to the world and the world to us.

THE CROSS AND THE WORLD

"WHEN I stand before the throne,
Dressed in beauty not my own,
When I see Thee as Thou art,
Love Thee with unsinning heart,
Then, Lord, shall I fully know—
Not till then—how much I owe."

"In the written word of prophecy we have something more permanent; to which you do well to pay attention—as to a lamp shining in a dimly lighted place—until day dawns and the morning star rises in your hearts." 2 Peter 1:19, Weymouth.

In studying this verse merely for its reference to prophecy, we miss a most important and practical lesson. Multitudes of people everywhere are groping in spiritual darkness. Many have a very meager knowledge of the Bible and of God. Others have heard, but because of the destructive criticism have lost their faith. Many of these people may be saved if in some manner their interest can be awakened and faith established in the reality of God and the divine origin of the Scriptures. Probably there is no other means within our reach so potent in accomplishing this as the prophecies. When men see all these divine predictions so accurately fulfilled hundreds and even thousands of years after they were made, they confess that there must be a God, and that the Scriptures must be a revelation from Him.

The word says we do well to take heed to these prophecies as unto a light that shines in a dark place, until the day dawns and the daystar arises in our hearts. After that glorious experience we do not need the prophecies to convince us that there is a God. He is in our hearts. We have the evidence in our own lives of the indwelling of Jesus Christ. When that radiant Morning Star, which is the harbinger of a new day, arises in our hearts, the day has dawned and a new life has begun. We know that Christ has come in the flesh.

"I pray that Christ may make His home in your hearts through your faith." Eph. 3:17, Weymouth. How expressive and significant that thought—that Christ will come and be at home in your heart! If He is at home there, you will not bring anything into that home which is displeasing to Him, or any company that would be objectionable to Him. It is important to note the emphasis the Scripture places on the *heart* —"until day dawns and the morning star rises in your hearts;" "that Christ may make His home in your hearts." Christianity is of the heart more than of the head. There may be a great deal of religion in the head, and but little Christianity in the heart. Christ may dwell in the head, the intellect; the historic Christ may be well known; but unless He dwells in the heart, there is no real contentment and satisfaction.

It is a wonderful thing to be able to say, "I have found that which perfectly satisfies my heart." Men are running to and fro in the earth, seeking out every human device, but no gratification of the physical senses or of the highest intellectual faculties can bring lasting peace and satisfaction. These can come only when there is peace and contentment in the heart.

There is nothing in all the world that can truly satisfy the heart except Jesus Christ. This is true because God made man for Himself, and at creation He provided a place in man's heart for Himself. In the heart of every intelligent human being there is a throne, and that being is never complete until the divine Master is seated on the throne. So men go wandering up and down in the earth, filled with disappointment, dissatisfaction, and unrest, until the throne of their hearts is occupied by the One for whom it was created. Then there is rest.

This is really the very essence of the Christian religion. "That Christ may make His home in your hearts." "Christ in you, the hope of glory." "I will dwell in them, and walk in them; and I will be their God, and they shall be My people." "Know ye not . . . that Jesus Christ is in you, except ye be reprobates?"

The genuineness and depth of our Christian experience may be tested by the vividness of our realization of the presence of Christ in us. Is Jesus real to you this moment, even more real than any human being? Then you have found One who perfectly satisfies your heart.

It does not seem to occur to many that it is the influence of the world still prevailing within that causes unrest and dissatisfaction, and a continual feverish desire and craving after the excitement of worldly associates and amusements. Thousands of young people are convicted of sins in their lives, and realize that they are not truly converted, and that there must be a change if they are saved, but they do not understand how the change is to be brought about. They feel a greater or less sense of condemnation over their indulgence in worldly pleasures, yet they do not see how they would find much satisfaction in living if they renounced all those things which, for the time being at least, give them satisfaction. But it is these very things of the world that rob them of peace and contentment.

The great majority of the young people today are filled with a spirit of restlessness, a feverish craving for a continual round of excitement. A character saturated with this spirit is necessarily selfish and shallow. It is the very opposite of that broad, noble, pure character which is the source of real contentment. "A life in Christ is a life of restfulness." The deeper and broader the river, as a rule, the more smoothly and calmly it flows on toward the sea. It is the little, turbulent, shallow stream that makes a great deal of fuss and noise. The same principle holds true in human character.

The great secret of peace, and happiness, and contentment, is not in material things, but in a Person. It is the world in the heart that causes discontent and unrest; it is Christ in the heart that brings peace and satisfaction. Therefore, the world must be cast out, and the Saviour enthroned. It is the only remedy, the only solution. And the method of making this great exchange is by way of the cross.

> "Each moment draw from earth away
>   My heart that lowly waits Thy call.
> Speak to my inmost soul, and say,
>   'I am thy love, thy God, thy all.'
> To feel Thy power, to hear Thy voice,
> To taste Thy love, is all my choice."

"God forbid that I should glory, save in the cross of our Lord Jesus Christ, by whom the world is crucified unto me, and I unto the world." Gal. 6:14.

A genuine Christian experience renders the possessor entirely independent of the world's sources of pleasure and enjoyment. God has a peace and joy and contentment as much higher than any the world can provide as heaven is higher than earth. He has clearly defined in His word the relation which should exist between His children and this world.

"Then said Jesus again unto them, I go My way, and ye shall seek Me, and shall die in your sins: whither I go, ye cannot come. Then said the Jews, Will He kill Himself? because He saith, Whither I go, ye cannot come. And He said unto them, Ye are from beneath; I am from above: ye are of this world; I am not of this world." John 8:21-23.

Jesus looked upon those people before Him and said, You will die in your sins and be lost. You may never come where I am going, because you are from beneath and belong to this world. I am from above, and belong to that better land. That is the relationship that Christ, our Master, sustained to this world. When we are born into His family, our affliction with this world is forever severed, and the world becomes our enemy, as it was His.

"If the world hate you, ye know that it hated Me before it hated you. If ye were of the world, the world would love his own: but because ye are not of the world, but I have chosen you out of the world, therefore the world hateth you." John 15:18, 19.

The world and a true Christian cannot be friends. No disciple of Christ can love the world which despised and denied and rejected his Master, and crucified Him between two thieves. The world hates them because they do not belong to the world, and can take no part in its activities.

"I have given them Thy word; and the world hath hated them, because they are not of the world, even as I am not of the world." John 17:14.

When Jesus was here, He loved sinners. He did not love their ways, their customs, or their practices; for they were of the world, and were hateful and abhorrent to Him. The spirit of the world, its ambitions, its pride and fashions, its pleasures and amusements, all were antagonistic to the very spirit and character of Jesus.

The apostle Paul mentions several striking characteristics of those who profess to be Christians in the last days, which makes it a perilous time. One of the sins he speaks of is pleasure loving. "Men shall be . . . lovers of pleasures more than lovers of God." The matter of pleasure, amusement, and entertainment doubtless occupies more of the attention of the civilized world today than any other subject. In the beginning, man was endowed by the Creator with the capacity and desire for enjoyment. It is certainly legitimate to desire and to enjoy good things for the body and for the mind. But there were bounds beyond which the enjoyment of these natural desires would be injurious to man's best interests. These natural bounds were defined in the instruction given to man by the Lord.

It has always been the supreme purpose of the devil to tempt man to go beyond these limits, in disobedience to God and to his own hurt. Temptation has been well defined as "the incitement of a natural desire to go beyond the bounds set by God." Had Adam and Eve been content to satisfy their natural desire for enjoyment by partaking of all the good things in the garden, and leaving the fruit on the forbidden tree alone, they would have experienced never-ending pleasure and happiness. By yielding to temptation and gratifying their desire to enjoy things beyond the bounds set by God, they opened the floodgates of weakness and perverted desire and sin and death upon the human race. Through all the ages the enemy has worked upon this human weakness with increasing success.

"The peril of the last days is not that men love pleasure, but that they love pleasure more than they love God."

This leads them to plunge more and more into those excesses which debase and ruin the moral and spiritual faculties. A mysterious and unreasonable infatuation, which is really madness, follows the indulgence of these desires contrary to the will of God. Many men today will saturate their bodies with such poisons as tobacco and alcoholic drinks, and regard this as one of their greatest sources of enjoyment. They cannot understand or believe that anyone can get much greater enjoyment from a clean mouth and a drink of pure water than they do from indulgence which brings degeneration of body, mind, and heart.

The psalmist wrote, "At Thy right hand there are pleasures forevermore." Only the true Christian knows the height and depth of genuine enjoyment which comes from the gratification of natural appetites and desires in harmony with the laws of God rather than in violation of them, which is idolatry.

"Neither be ye idolaters, as were some of them; as it is written, The people sat down to eat and drink, and rose up to play."

Who has not seen this enacted many times among professed Christians in our day? In all the ages, Satan has had two great weapons of aggressive warfare. First, he has persecuted and sought to destroy by violent means the followers of Christ. Second, failing in this, he has schemed in every conceivable way to obliterate the line between the church and the world, introducing into the church those selfish and worldly practices which weaken her members and destroy her spirituality.

The church never plunges into backsliding and apostasy at a single bound. It is by a gradual and almost imperceptible yielding to the pressure of the world and the sophistry of the enemy, that the church drifts away from the true standards of righteousness. The only successful barrier against this fatal encroachment of the world upon the church is the cross of Christ. Let Christ be lifted up, the cross exalted, and the bitter hatred and animosity of the world are aroused.

The Saviour's parable of the rich man and Lazarus furnishes an impressive lesson on the fatal blindness of those who shape their lives only with a view to the enjoyment of this world.

"The rich man claimed to be a son of Abraham, but he was separated from Abraham by an impassable gulf,—a character wrongly developed. Abraham served God, following His word in faith and obedience. But the rich man was unmindful of God, and of the needs of suffering humanity. The great gulf fixed between him and Abraham was the gulf of disobedience.

"There are many today who are following the same course. Though church members, they are unconverted. They may take part in the church service, they may chant the psalm, 'As the hart panteth after the water brooks, so panteth my soul after Thee, O God;' but they testify to a falsehood. They are no more righteous in God's sight than is the veriest sinner.

"The soul that longs after the excitement of worldly pleasure, the mind that is full of love for display, cannot serve God. Like the rich man in the parable, such a one has no inclination to war against the lust of the flesh. He longs to indulge appetite. He chooses the atmosphere of sin. He is suddenly snatched away by death, and he goes down to the grave with the character formed during his lifetime in copartnership with satanic agencies. In the grave he has no power to choose anything, be it good or evil; for in the day when a man dies, his thoughts perish.

"When the voice of God awakes the dead, he will come from the grave with the same appetites and passions, the same likes and dislikes, that he cherished when living. God works no miracle to re-create a man who would not be re-created when he was granted every opportunity and provided with every facility. During his lifetime he took no delight in God, nor found pleasure in His service. His character is not in harmony with God, and he could not be happy in the heavenly family."—*"Christ's Object Lessons," pp. 269, 270.*

Surely those church members are in great peril who are lovers of pleasure more than lovers of God. If they cannot obtain happiness and satisfaction from Christ sufficient to overcome their craving for the dance, the theater, and other worldly amusements, and their lives should be suddenly snatched away, it is utterly inconsistent to believe they are prepared for heaven. If a man dies while his mind is wrought up with the exciting scenes of a theater, it is logical to believe that in the resurrection his first thought will not be of the Saviour or of heaven, but of the silly unrealities of the stage or screen.

A man's character undergoes no change while he is in the grave. If he dies in a dance hall or a bowling alley, or while indulging in some other selfish amusement merely to gratify his carnal appetites and tendencies, when he comes forth from the grave it will be with the same character. But the things which have been his joy and pleasure will not be found in heaven, for the law of heaven is unselfish love and service for others, rather than living to please oneself. He would not be happy in heaven, for he would not find there the things which are his chief delight here.

"Love not the world, neither the things that are in the world. If any man love the world, the love of the Father is not in him." 1 John 2:15.

The Lord could not have spoken more plainly than this. And yet a great many Christians seem to have the idea that the world is all right, and the things of the world are desirable, and it is legitimate to get all the pleasure we can out of them, only so one does not indulge in the grosser sins. But the Bible teaches exactly contrary to such an idea. God did not love the customs and practices, the pride and vanity, the fashions and amusements, of the world, but He did love the people. The Scripture says, "Set your affection on things above, not on things on the earth." We may love the things of that better world. They are ours. We are here for a short time; and as soon as our work is done, we shall go there, where we belong, to inherit the things our Father has prepared for us.

I meet a professed Christian who loves the pleasures and fashions of the world, and has a spirit of unrest and craving for its exciting associations and amusements, and talk with him about the cross of Christ and the life of victory and peace, but he is almost certain to say, "I do not understand what you mean by all this talk about the victorious life. I cannot see anything real to it, nor how you obtain it." Truly, "the god of this world hath blinded the minds of them which believe not."

A young lady recently said to me, "If I were to be a really pious, genuine Christian, it would take all the joy out of life." It is true that real fellowship with Christ soon destroys the desire and the capacity for enjoying the follies and selfish indulgences of the carnal nature.

To many the life of a true Christian seems a slow, dull, stupid affair. They cannot see how he can endure life deprived of what they call a good time—no theater, no dance, no cards, no movies—what a dull life that must be! On the other hand, the true Christian regards all those things as shallow and empty and unsatisfying.

Sometimes young people are inclined to think that all their pleasures and amusements are condemned simply because they have lost their attraction for the older people who disapprove of them. They say, "When I get old, I shall no longer care for these things either, but now I am young, and I want to enjoy life as I go along."

Sometime ago I went with an earnest Christian young man to visit a school. In speaking to the students I said: "Some of you young men may not be convinced when we tell you that the amusements and pleasures of the world do not satisfy the heart. The world is bidding high for your lives, and it may not be easy for you to realize how empty and deceptive and valueless is all it has to offer. You may think that some of us have never had those things which appeal to you and which your heart is set on possessing, and that we are speaking only theoretically and are really undervaluing the things of the world.

"You may have an ambition to get into the world and acquire wealth and position and honor. My friend, who is sitting here before you, is in a position to speak of these things from experience. He was until recently a prosperous businessman. He was probably making as much money as any of you would ever make if you devoted your lives to seeking wealth. He was a member of the Chamber of Commerce, the Rotary Club, the Kiwanis Club, and a thirty-third-degree Mason. He had a host of friends, a beautiful home, a thriving business, and about every prospect a young man could ask for.

"But he heard this great message of the soon coming of Jesus to set up His everlasting kingdom, and in it he heard a call to lay aside every worldly ambition, and let Christ reign supreme in his heart. Like the apostle Paul, he counted 'all things but loss for the excellency of the knowledge of Christ Jesus' his Lord. In order to prepare for active service in the cause of Christ, he disposed of all his worldly business, and severed every association that would interfere with his success in the work of soul winning. His testimony about the comparative values of the world and the Saviour should have weight with you, and I wish you would talk with him about it."

They came to him, and he talked with them simply and sensibly and lovingly. He got down on his knees and prayed with them and for them, and led them to the foot of the cross. It was a wonderful experience for the students, and a precious experience for the young man. After two days he said to me, "These two days have been the happiest and most wonderful days of my life."

Jesus satisfies the heart. When He comes and fills our hearts, there is no longer that longing and craving for the excitement of worldly amusements. There is no place in the heart for self-gratification and selfish indulgence. The presence of Christ brings in the pure, unselfish atmosphere of heaven, which is infinitely sweeter and more satisfying.

I am aware that many professed Christians still have these desires for worldly pleasures. They are infatuated with the moving-picture theaters. They tell me how beautiful and instructive they are, and what excellent lessons they teach, and they tell me other things which betray the true character of those places of amusement. There is a moral infatuation, a spiritual blindness and stupor, possessing those who find enjoyment in the things that are not of God. When they experience a spiritual awakening, they often tell me candidly of the effect of such indulgence upon their Christian life.

Recently a friend related something of his experience. He told me he had always rather prided himself on being sensible and conservative and broad-minded in the matter of amusements. Occasionally, when one of the so-called high-class films was advertised, he and his wife attended. They were persuaded to attend one which was widely advertised as a grand picture, which taught exalted moral lessons, and made the most thrilling and lasting impressions for good. He declared that it was truly a marvelous production. It must have taken a prodigious amount of work and cost a vast sum of money.

I asked if he approved of it, and would advise others to go and see it. He replied emphatically in the negative, for he said that while much of the picture was beautiful and attractive, scenes were displayed which were unspeakably vile and disgusting.

However refined and cultured and pure people may consider themselves, it is inconceivable that they could sit and absorb such scenes without suffering a moral paralysis, a blunting and benumbing of the finest, purest sensibilities of the soul. Thus they drift, little by little, farther from the true standards of modesty and purity, until they fall an easy prey to the enemy.

The film alluded to was based upon a historical incident recorded in the Bible. About thirty-five hundred years ago God led a people out of Egypt. They had been in bondage for scores of years, and were enveloped in spiritual ignorance and darkness. God led them forth by a mighty hand and an outstretched arm, and in a few days they reached Mt. Sinai. God descended upon the mountain and revealed Himself in the most sublime display of divine power and glory the world has ever seen. He declared that moral law which is a transcript of His character. The vast multitude of men and women trembled with fear and apprehension. But Moses, their great leader, was called up into the mountain, and during his long absence the people, led by the ungodly and pleasure-loving among them, fell back into the awful darkness of abominable idolatry, and made a golden calf. They engaged in the degrading practices of the idol-worshiping heathen, whom God proposed to destroy before them.

When Moses came down from the mountain and saw the terrible apostasy of the people, he was filled with indignation. At his command the loyal servants of God took swords and visited summary judgment upon those who had participated in this disgraceful debauchery. Three thousand souls perished before the camp was purged of its uncleanness.

If the course of those poor people just emerging from a century or more of abject slavery was so reprehensible in the sight of God, what must He think of men and women living two thousand years this side of Calvary, who pay their money to see the immoral and revolting scenes of Israel's apostasy reproduced on the screen? How can our spiritual sensibilities be so stupefied and paralyzed that in these last solemn hours of probationary time we can take pleasure in attending for mere amusement those places where the name of God is blasphemed, and a profane and sacrilegious use is made of His holy word?

The one in whose heart Jesus Christ is really enthroned has no desire for such entertainment. He is not constantly craving those associations and amusements which stifle the voice of conscience, and unfit him for the work of saving souls from ruin. God has given him something infinitely better than the world can give. I have never seen a church member who gave evidence of genuine conversion and was enthusiastic in the service of God and eager to win souls, who maintained for a moment that he was blessed or benefited by attending any worldly places of amusement.

Can you imagine an angel from glory getting satisfaction and joy out of the theater, card playing, or the movies? If Christ were here, could He take part in these gaieties and follies and frivolities of the world? How can we do the things which in our hearts we know Christ would not do, nor want His followers to do? If we desire to do here the things He disapproves, how can we expect Him to welcome us to that better world, whose inhabitants delight only in His will?

Suppose we should learn that a young woman of our acquaintance has been the victim of a terrible tragedy. Her husband has been foully murdered by wicked men. We go to her home to console and comfort her. When we reach the house, we find her sitting in the room, laughing and jesting and being entertained by a group of men. We inquire who they are, and she admits that they are the men who murdered her husband. It is unthinkable, and yet it illustrates what we who profess to be Christ's disciples do when we love and court the world and crave the excitement and amusement it provides. We are loving and seeking that world which hated and crucified our Master. To the extent that we love and seek the world and affiliate with it, we are false to Christ.

The wise man says, "Keep thy heart with all diligence; for out of it are the issues of life." Prov. 4:23.

The heart will be the throne of either Christ or the great enemy of Christ. We must choose which one we will have to reign in our lives.

Has Christ been reigning in your life, and have you found that relationship to Him that brings peace and contentment into your heart? You may find it at the cross.

110

THE FACE OF CHRIST

Of all the themes which have inspired the pens of devoutly spiritual poets and the voices of consecrated singers down through the ages, no other equals that of the face of Christ. A few years ago it was said that no other song known to the human race was so universally sung as the "Glory Song."

> "When, by the gift of His infinite grace,
> I am accorded in heaven a place,
> Just to be there and to look on His face,
> Will through the ages be glory for me."

There is a deeper reason for this instinctive fascination in the face of Jesus than many realize. The apostle Paul makes a profoundly significant statement in his letter to the Corinthian believers: "God, who commanded the light to shine out of darkness, hath shined in our hearts, to give the light of the knowledge of the glory of God in the face of Jesus Christ."

Here is a revelation worthy of our deepest meditation and prolonged contemplation. The truth suggested is so sublime and exalted that the inspired apostle must needs, for an adequate illustration, reach far back to the hour of creation, when "the worlds were framed by the word of God." This world was surrounded by a pall of darkness unpenetrated by a ray from sun or star. Where there was no light, there was no life; all was darkness and death. Then God said, "Let there be light: and there was light."

This world in its state of chaos and darkness fitly represents the life of the sinner. He is described as

111

"having the understanding darkened, being alienated from the life of God," an alien "from the commonwealth of Israel," a stranger "from the covenants of promise, having no hope, and without God in the world." While man was in this deplorable and lost condition, God looked upon him with infinite pity and love. In His eternal plan He had provided a means by which the darkness might be dispelled from the sinner, as it was from this chaotic world. Jesus came as the Sun of Righteousness, and life springs up where the light shines. The light of the knowledge of the glory of God is in the face of Jesus Christ.

And so one of old was inspired to write, "They looked unto Him, and were lightened: and their faces were not ashamed." Numberless times lost men and women have looked up into the face of Christ, and their faces have been lightened, and have reflected something of the glory of God. Others of His saints have looked out of the darkest night of sorrow, or persecution, or loss, or the very shadow of death, and the light has shined into their hearts and inspired them to sing:

"O for a vision of Jesus,
 O for a glimpse of His face;
Radiant with heavenly beauty,
 Beaming with heavenly grace."

A vision of His face seen with the eye of faith alone has inspired men to work and pray, to live and sacrifice, to suffer and die, in anticipation of a future life where they can bask in the light of His countenance forevermore.

"Someday the silver cord will break,
 And I no more as now shall sing;
But, O, the joy when I shall wake
 Within the palace of the King!
And I shall see Him face to face,
And tell the story, Saved by grace."

What is there to be learned by looking into the face of Jesus? What is the light of the knowledge of the glory of God that shines in the face of Jesus Christ? The glory of God is His character. When He showed Moses His glory, He proclaimed, "The Lord, The Lord God, merciful and gracious, long-suffering, and abundant in goodness and truth." As we see this character reflected in the face of Christ, our hearts long to be clothed with the same pure and holy attributes, and God satisfies that longing by the transformation of our lives.

As we study what the Holy Scriptures reveal concerning the face of Christ, we realize that this is not a mere abstract theory, but a practical work wrought by the Holy Spirit.

"We all, with open face beholding as in a glass the glory of the Lord, are changed into the same image from glory to glory, even as by the Spirit of the Lord."

In every severe trial of our lives, in every crisis through which we pass, the strength and wisdom and courage we need will be revealed and imparted if we look steadfastly into the face of Jesus.

HIS FACE ILLUMINED

"After six days Jesus taketh Peter, James, and John his brother, and bringeth them up into a high mountain apart, and was transfigured before them: and His face did shine as the sun." Another disciple informs us that it was "as He prayed" that "the fashion of His countenance was altered."

This was the divine illumination that came to Jesus, our example, as He communed with God in the solitude of the mountain. He had come to earth to seek and to save the lost. He had no personal ambitions to satisfy, no desire for selfish pleasure or sensual gratification. His one burden was to save lost souls. For them He prayed, and for the presence of the mighty convicting Spirit, that men might be awakened and converted. As He prayed, He was illumined.

"It came to pass, that on the next day, when they were come down from the hill, much people met Him." He seemed to be surrounded by that mysterious heavenly influence which compels men to look up from the gross, material things of this world, and reach out after God. This divine illumination is the outshining of His love.

Alone in the mountain, Moses prayed for a fuller revelation of God. "I beseech Thee, show me Thy glory." When he came down from the mountain, his face was so radiant with that inner light that the people feared, for they recognized in him the presence of God.

It is not more extensive learning or brilliant scholarship or eloquent oratory that is needed today so much as the divine illumination of the soul that results from mountaintop prayer and communion with God, looking into the face of Jesus until some of the light of the knowledge of the glory of God is reflected from our own.

HIS STEADFAST FACE

"It came to pass, when the time was come that He should be received up, He steadfastly set His face to go to Jerusalem."

Jesus experienced the greatest joy day by day in His blessed ministry of love. To break the bands of sin and relieve those oppressed by the devil, to restore sight to blind eyes, hearing to deaf ears, and health to all that were suffering, was His life. And yet, all through the years He had been conscious of the shadow of Calvary. He had borne the cross every day of His life—your cross and mine. Now the time had come for the consummation of the eternal plan that He should lay down His life as the sinner's substitute.

It was a sorrowful way, but there was no shrinking on His part. He set His face steadfastly to go to Jerusalem, knowing that it meant bitter persecution and reproach, ending in rejection, condemnation, and the ignominy and disgrace of the crucifixion. The disciples had never before seen that look on His face—so stern, resolute, and unwavering that they hesitated to disturb His meditations.

It is that steadfast purpose in the face of Christ to carry out the divine will even to the limit of Gethsemane and Calvary that we are to appropriate in hours of darkness and suffering for His sake.

I stood before a thousand Indians who had come out of the darkness and superstition of virtual heathenism under terrible persecution. Many had been robbed of their possessions, others had been beaten and stoned and imprisoned, and had seen friends shot down or brutally done to death for their faith in Christ. There were eighteen schools clustered about the mission, and this was a general meeting of the believers. The representatives of one school had not yet arrived, and when they came, they presented a spectacle that might make angels weep. Following their devoted teacher, they marched to the front of the congregation and stood in line before us. They had been the objects of an inhuman attack by a fanatical mob. Men, women, and children had been beaten with clubs and stones, and were covered with wounds and bruises and blood. And then they sang:

> "I must have the Saviour with me,
> For I dare not walk alone;
> I must feel His presence near me,
> And His arm around me thrown.
>
> "I must have the Saviour with me,
> In the onward march of life,
> In the tempest and the sunshine,
> Through the battle and the strife.
>
> "Then my soul shall fear no ill,
> Let Him lead me where He will,
> I will go without a murmur,
> And His footsteps follow still."

115

These poor Indians were just emerging from generations of cruel oppression, and the densest spiritual and intellectual ignorance and darkness; yet who can say that the Spirit of God had not given these simple children of the Andes a glimpse of the steadfast face of Jesus? One who knows them cannot doubt that they have caught some rays of the light of the knowledge of the glory of God revealed in the face of Jesus Christ.

HIS EARTH-STAINED FACE

What a startling and amazing word to use in our contemplation of the face of Jesus! Let us think of it reverently.

"Then cometh Jesus with them into a place called Gethsemane, and saith unto the disciples, Sit ye here, while I go and pray yonder. And He took with Him Peter and the two sons of Zebedee, and began to be sorrowful and very heavy. Then saith He unto them, My soul is exceeding sorrowful, even unto death: tarry ye here, and watch with Me. And He went a little farther, and fell on His face, and prayed, saying, O My Father, if it be possible, let this cup pass from Me: nevertheless not as I will, but as Thou wilt."

It was here that the final struggle began which ended only with the triumphant cry from the cross, "It is finished," when the eternal victory was won. He was lying prostrate with His face pressing the ground which His own word had spoken into existence. The mighty waves of the darkness were rolling over Him, but He trod "the wine press alone; and of the people there was none with" Him.

> " 'Tis midnight; and on Olive's brow
> The star is dimmed that lately shone:
> 'Tis midnight; in the garden, now,
> The suffering Saviour prays alone."

Well may we pray for discernment, for here indeed is the light of the knowledge of the glory of God shining in the face of Jesus.

It is the light of that love which "hopeth all things, endureth all things," that sinners may be reconciled to God.

As His disciples, we may expect scorn and hatred and persecution from the world, and we may go to our Gethsemane in our conflict against self and the powers of darkness; but there is light and comfort and eternal hope reflected from the dusty face of Christ.

"The garden, where of old our guilt began,
Wrought death and pain;
But this, where Jesus prays by night for man,
Brings life and joy again."

THE BRUISED FACE

"The men that held Jesus mocked Him, and smote Him. And when they had blindfolded Him, they struck Him on the face."

How can one contemplate this scene without a sense of inexpressible shame that any member of the human family could thus treat its greatest Benefactor? Even had Jesus been a vile and depraved criminal, no good end would have been attained by such inhuman abuse. It is no wonder that they covered His face before they struck Him. The wonder is that the unsullied purity and majestic nobility of His face did not smite them with an awful conviction.

What a startling revelation this is of the deadly, malignant nature of sin, and its power to envelop the soul in spiritual and moral midnight! The light of the knowledge of the glory of God was shining from that face, and they drew back the fist and struck it. Oh, appalling darkness and depravity that results from rejecting light! It was to save us from that darkness and cruelty that He was suffering. "He was wounded for our transgressions, He was bruised for our iniquities: the chastisement of our peace was upon Him; and with His stripes we are healed."

How can we look upon that holy face, so marred

117

and bruised for our sins, without experiencing a fierce indignation against sin, and forming a great resolution to wage unceasing warfare against it by the grace of God, both in our lives and in the world?

And how the cruel marks of Gethsemane and Calvary should endear the Saviour to us! The story is told of a little girl who one day noticed that her mother's hands were not smooth and beautiful like the hands of her little friend's mother, but were rough and ugly. She asked, "Mother, why are your hands so dark and rough?" The mother replied, "When you were a little babe learning to walk, you fell into the open fireplace, and in an instant your clothes were all on fire. Mother ran and caught you up, and put the fire out with her hands. Since then her hands have been black and ugly and scarred, as you see them." The little one looked at the marred hands a moment, and said, "Mother, I think yours are the most beautiful hands I ever saw."

"Marred more than any man's, yet there's no place
  In the wide universe but gains new grace,
  Richer and fuller, from that marred face!

"O Saviour Christ, those precious wounds of Thine
  Make doubly precious these poor wounds of mine;
  Teach me to die, with Thee, the death divine.

"Heaven beckons me, I press me toward the mark
  Of my high calling—Hark, He calls, O hark!
  That wounded Face moves toward me through the dark."
                                        —C. A. Fox.

Someday those who "with His stripes" have been healed, will have the privilege of telling Him how beautiful are the wounds in His hands and feet and side. One of the ancient prophets looked forward to that day. Jesus was not then "despised and rejected of men," but "His glory covered the heavens, and the earth was full of His praise. And His brightness was as the light; and He had bright beams out of His side: and there was the hiding of His power." Instead of the blood flowing from His pierced side, the scar will radiate streams of light. "The tokens of His humiliation are His highest honor; through the eternal ages the wounds of Calvary will show forth His praise, and declare His power."

THE DEAD FACE

"Another Scripture saith, They shall look on Him whom they pierced."

It is a solemn and sorrowful thing to look on the face of our dead. No language can express our pain, though we have done all in our power for the departed one. A story is told of a little girl who in an accident was thrown into the river. Instantly her little brother, only eight years old, plunged into the water to rescue her. He struggled heroically, but in vain, and was barely saved himself. As he stood beside the little casket, he put his hands on her cheeks and with the tears streaming down his face he said, "O sister, I would have saved you if I could! You know I would have saved you if I could!" How a mother mourns over the little child who has done nothing for her, but for whom she has done everything!

But there is One hanging lifeless on the cross, who has done everything for us, and for whom we have done nothing. What inexpressible grief should melt our hearts in contemplation of such an unfeeling crime as ours! Surely we should "mourn for Him, as one mourneth for his only son." And we may well take our place by the side of the Roman centurion, who stood beneath the cross, and, looking up into that face, so calm and peaceful and loving even in death, say with him, "Truly this was the Son of God."

Mr. Moody once said that when Jesus ascended up on high, all He left of Himself in this world was the pool of blood at the foot of the cross. For four thousand years the children of men had looked forward to the hour when the Lamb of God should shed His blood for the remission of sins. Now that shed blood is accessible to every sinner in the world—but only at the foot of the cross.

> "There is a fountain filled with blood,
>   Drawn from Immanuel's veins;
> And sinners plunged beneath that flood
>   Lose all their guilty stains.

> "The dying thief rejoiced to see
>   That fountain in his day;
> And there may I, though vile as he,
>   Wash all my sins away."

THE FACE OF THE KING

Next to Christ's death on the cross, the great theme of the Bible is His second coming in glory. His promise is, "I go to prepare a place for you. And if I go and prepare a place for you, I will come again, and receive you unto Myself; that where I am, there ye may be also." It is this promise of His coming that gives emphasis to all the warnings and exhortations and promises of the Bible. In the last chapter of the Holy Scriptures is the solemn, threefold announcement:

"Behold I come quickly: blessed is he that keepeth the sayings of the prophecy of this book."

"Behold, I come quickly; and My reward is with Me, to give every man according as his work shall be."

"He which testifieth these things saith, Surely I come quickly."

The grandeur of that event no human pen can describe. He will come in all His glory, and in the glory of the Father and of all the holy angels. "Every eye shall see Him, and they also which pierced Him: and all kindreds of the earth shall wail because of Him."

What shall we do when we look up and see Him coming, before whose face the heavens shall flee away?

"The heaven departed as a scroll when it is rolled together; and every mountain and island were moved out of their places. And the kings of the earth, and the great men, and the rich men, and the chief captains, and the mighty men, and every bondman, and every free man, hid themselves in the dens and in the rocks of the mountains; and said to the mountains and rocks, Fall on us, and hide us from the face of Him that sitteth on the throne, and from the wrath of the Lamb."

How dreadful that I should cry for a mountain to roll upon me and hide me from that face which was marred and bruised and spit upon and crowned with thorns that I might be eternally saved! How incomprehensible is the infatuation of sin, how fatal its mysterious madness!

But not all the children of men will seek to hide from His face in that great day.

"He will swallow up death in victory; and the Lord God will wipe away tears from off all faces; and the rebuke of His people shall He take away from off all the earth: for the Lord hath spoken it. And it shall be said in that day, Lo, this is our God; we have waited for Him, and He will save us: this is the Lord; we have waited for Him, we will be glad and rejoice in His salvation."

They have been waiting for Him. They have gazed often and long into His blessed face with the eye of faith. As they have set forth in His footsteps to carry the gospel to perishing men, they have looked into His illumined face. They have learned the secret of prayer until the "light of His heavenly love" shines in their faces, and they have become channels for that mysterious power that attracts sinners to the cross.

When called to face self-denial and sacrifice, they have looked into His steadfast face, and heaven approached as the things of the world receded.

When required to carry the heavy burden of suffering and shame for others, they have looked upon the dusty face, and remembered that Jesus trod the way before them, and they gladly follow Him.

121

When hated, and persecuted, and cast out for His sake, they have looked upon the bruised face, and gathered strength to endure, and learned to rejoice that they were counted worthy to suffer with Him.

When tempted by the allurements of sin and the pleasures of the world, they have looked at His face in death, and realized anew that "the sting of death is sin," and have seen, even in that still face, the light of the knowledge of the glory of God, pointing them to a better world, even a heavenly.

And when the time seems long, and the way seems steep and lonely, they have looked up at the victorious face of the coming King, and have been cheered on with the hope of eternal reward.

Friend, are you acquainted with Jesus? Have you seen Him uplifted on the cross for your redemption? Is He real to you? Do you know with what infinite patience and love His face is turned toward you, seeking to win you from death to life? He is coming soon—very soon. There will be a glorious new earth, with sin forever banished, and no sickness, sorrow, or death. All His true children who have obeyed Him and made His service first in this world, will be there.

"AND THEY SHALL SEE HIS FACE."

"Face to face! O, blissful moment!
Face to face—to see and know;
Face to face with my Redeemer,
Jesus Christ, who loves me so."

TEACH Services, Inc.
P U B L I S H I N G

We invite you to view the complete
selection of titles we publish at:
www.TEACHServices.com

We encourage you to write us
with your thoughts about this,
or any other book we publish at:
info@TEACHServices.com

TEACH Services' titles may be purchased in
bulk quantities for educational, fund-raising,
business, or promotional use.
bulksales@TEACHServices.com

Finally, if you are interested in seeing
your own book in print, please contact us at:
publishing@TEACHServices.com

We are happy to review your manuscript at no charge.